GOD BLESS
AMERICA *AGAIN*

A PROPHETIC PERSPECTIVE

ALLEN JACKSON

GOD BLESS AMERICA *AGAIN*

A PROPHETIC PERSPECTIVE

BOUND TRANSCRIPTS
SERMONS IN BOOK FORM

TABLE OF CONTENTS

AN INTRODUCTION TO THE
BOUND TRANSCRIPTS

The contents of this book are taken directly from the transcripts of Pastor Allen Jackson's sermons at World Outreach Church in Murfreesboro, Tennessee.

In bringing them to book form, our primary objective is to maintain the full integrity of the message, as it was delivered in the sanctuary. This means, for the overwhelming majority of the text, it is a verbatim transcription. In sections where the oral presentation didn't translate effectively to written word, only minor edits were made to reduce confusion for the reader.

Also, from time to time in the text, you'll see paragraphs written in blue letters. These are sections where Pastor Allen has interjected an aside, or added a few extra thoughts to the idea after the sermon was delivered.

These sermons contain powerful and timeless truths from Scripture. We hope you enjoy reading them and trust that, as you choose to cooperate with the Spirit of the Lord, He will unleash freedom, peace, strength, love, hope, forgiveness, and restoration in your life.

God bless you on your journey.

AN INTRODUCTION TO
GOD BLESS AMERICA AGAIN

Edward Everit Hale wrote a short story entitled "Man Without a Country". He describes a young man who in a moment of great emotion shouts, "I wish I may never hear of the United States again." The consequences for the young man are tragic. His wish is granted—he never again sets foot on American soil, nor is anyone allowed to speak to him of his country. The remaining years of his life are filled with regret at the opportunities lost.

If we ignore, or redesign our history to placate the whim of popular sentiment, we will forfeit much. Our nation was founded upon biblical principles by people with a desire to find an opportunity to worship the God of Abraham, Isaac, and Jacob, without interference from king or state church.

Our great freedoms and liberties have emerged from a Judeo-Christian worldview, derived from the Bible. Each generation must determine which principles will guide us. This is a tremendous responsibility, for it only requires three generations for an idea to be lost. If we fail to embrace those things which brought us liberty and freedom, and to teach them to the next generation, we are abandoning our responsibilities.

History is often seen as burdensome, dry, or laborious. I disagree. Understanding how God has consistently blessed America—time and again pouring out upon us His grace and mercy—

provides hope for the days ahead. We cannot afford to forget our past—good and bad—or we will forfeit the best opportunities of our future.

We are a people with a country! We are a people with a God! We are a people with a future, bright with possibility, if we will once again turn in humility and honor Almighty God. God bless America, again!

Allen Jackson

Senior Pastor of World Outreach Church

GOD BLESS AMERICA AGAIN

GOD BLESS AMERICA AGAIN

There's no question that God has blessed our nation. We wouldn't be the people we are, and we would not have enjoyed the blessings we have had without the grace and the mercy of God being showered upon us. But we're in a season where we need a visitation from the Lord, again. We need His wisdom and His grace and His mercy, and the incubator for our nation experiencing that—the instigator of that—is the Church. The problems we face are not political in their origin; they're not medical or scientific. The root of the problems that we face, the root of what's causing the anxiety in our streets and the sickness and disease across our nation, begins at a spiritual level. I don't expect the secularists to believe that, but if the Church doesn't believe that, we're doomed, because the response of the Church is critical. Unfortunately, we have misunderstood. We have thought sitting in church and being polite was the same thing as seeking God. But if we will change, the good news is that we have the power to bring about a different outcome. We don't need an army. We don't need Congress to vote. We don't need an election. If we will humble ourselves, God will move, and our children and our grandchildren will get a different future. It's an amazing thing.

But I want to submit to you that we've lost our sense of the fundamentals of the Church. Church with a capital "C", not just our congregation. Who we are to be, what is necessary to believe in, and what our role in the world is to be all seems to be muddied. We're confused. It's easy to become bewildered today amidst the array of answers that are available in the marketplace of ideas, because a Judeo-Christian worldview isn't celebrated. In fact, there's a temptation just to throw up our hands and declare all of them valid options. That's the reason that pluralism oftentimes leads to relativism—to the idea that there really is no overarching, objective truth, but only a variety and whole menu list of subjective beliefs.

It's important to clarify this in our hearts and our minds, because Scripture is clear what happens if we fail to fulfill the purpose for which God instituted the Church. Be certain of this: The Church is God's idea, but our primary goal as Christ-followers is not to go to Heaven, but to do the will of God while we're on earth. God will take care of our eternity if we will commit ourselves to fully doing the will of God while we're on earth, while we're under the sun. Matthew describes what happens if we fail to fulfill God's purpose:

"You are the salt of the earth. But if the salt loses its saltiness, how can it be made salty again? It is no longer good for anything, except to be thrown out and trampled underfoot."

MATTHEW 5:13

Now, lest we despair (because if you just watch the evening news, or you took the temperature of our current culture, you *can* be filled with despair), there is significant historical and biblical evidence that cultures can be renewed, even those that have been the most corrupt and the most intractable. But if we're to restore our world, if we're to see God's restoration, we first have to shake off the comfortable notion that Christianity is merely a personal experience—that it's primarily just about your private life. The poet, John Dunne wrote, "No man is an island." And one of the great myths of our day is that we are islands, that our decisions are personal, and that no one has the right to tell us what to do in our private lives. We too quickly forget that every private decision contributes to the moral and cultural climate in which we all live. It ripples out in ever-widening circles, first in our personal lives, and then into our family lives, and then into the broader society. It's startling. Truthfully, it's alarming the degree to which moral clarity is hard to find in our schools, in our universities, in the halls of government, and tragically, even in many pulpits—the places where patriotism, honor, and courage are needed the most. Instead of civics, we've been teaching our students moral ambivalence and cynicism. They're routinely taught to believe that America represents nothing more than one of many different, equal nations—that there's no such thing as a better or worse culture, only morally equivalent ones. It's a lie—that cultural values different from our own, regardless of their substance, need to be celebrated in the spirit of tolerance, and that, all things considered, Americans have at least as much to answer for as to be proud of.

I never imagined when I was in college that a degree in history was going to be as significant as it is today in sorting through truth and deception. This is a sign of moral relativism at its worst. It undermines love of country and provides intellectual insulation to our enemies. It represents a tremendous threat to our long-term national security, and to be honest, it has to stop. And I believe it has to stop in the hearts of those of us who consider ourselves to be Christ-followers.

Moral clarity does not require an uncritical evaluation of our own history and western ideals. Patriotism is not crude nationalism. Injustice isn't the sin of shortcomings. They're certainly a part of the American story, and we have to say so. But a fair and serious study of our own history shows that our nation, without a doubt, has been and continues to be a great force for good in the modern world. You and I are heirs to a precious legacy, but the perpetuation of our nation is not assured.

We heard Mike Huckabee very recently say that he was concerned that we might not celebrate another birthday as a nation with freedom and liberty for all. Pericles said to his fellow Athenians—I know you read lots of Greek history—"Your country has a right to your services in sustaining the glories of her position; these are a common source of pride to you all and you cannot decline the burdens of empire and still expect to share its honors." An America that declines its burdens—a nation that is indifferent as to why it fights—will deteriorate, will decline, and ultimately will fail. That's the prospect we face. And what I'm submitting to you, and the purpose for these lessons, is that we are standing on a precipice—the dividing line—and the time has come for us to begin to remember our heritage and the sacrifices that have been made for us so that we might enjoy the privileges that we have today. They have not come without cost, and they won't be extended to the generations who follow us without sacrifice on our part. We cannot, with a clear conscience, gobble up the blessings of God and ignore our responsibilities towards obedience and faithfulness and imagine that those blessings will be extended to those who follow us.

I. LESSONS FROM SCRIPTURE

I'd like to start with some lessons from Scripture. They're rather simple observations and generalizations, about the picture of Scripture that we have.

A. INTERNAL PROBLEMS A GREATER THREAT THAN EXTERNAL PROBLEMS

The first is that internal problems are a greater threat to our well-being than external problems. External enemies were never the greatest threat to the people of God. The Canaanites weren't the greatest threat to the Israelites. The Philistines weren't the greatest threat. It was what was within their hearts that posed the greatest threat, and our greatest threat today is not a secular culture, or a progressive ideology, or another nation in the world. The greatest threat to our future is what's within the hearts of those of us who imagine ourselves to be Christ-followers.

B. GOD'S PEOPLE, WITH EXPRESSIONS OF RELIGION/FAITH, WANDER FROM THE TRUTH

The second lesson would be that God's people, with expressions of religion and faith as a part of their daily routine, often wander from God's truth. You can be fully engaged in religious activities, language, and holidays and stray far away from the truth of God. Our Bible is filled with those reminders.

C. GOD INVITES US TO REPENT

Thirdly, God invites us to repent. This lesson isn't about someone else. We have to start saying that *we* will take a step of repentance. We're not going to make a note for somebody else. We're going to say, "We will repent."

D. REFUSAL TO CHANGE RESULTS IN JUDGMENT

Fourthly, a refusal to change—if we refuse repentance, if we stubbornly stand and point at our self-righteousness, the result in Scripture is typically God's judgment.

II. SINS OF AMERICA

I want to take a minute and look at the prophets and see if we can understand with a bit more clarity the sins of contemporary America. There's a lot of discussion around that these days, and I believe the Scripture speaks to it with clarity—shocking clarity.

I've often said I think Jeremiah had one of the toughest job descriptions in the Bible. He was a prophet in Jerusalem when the judgment of God was inevitably coming upon the people. The Babylonians were headed to Jerusalem, and Jeremiah spent his life delivering that message and watching what was coming.

Let's look at Jeremiah chapter 5:

> *A horrible and shocking thing has happened in the land:*
> *The prophets prophesy lies, the priests rule by their own*
> *authority, and my people love it this way. But what will you*
> *do in the end?*

JEREMIAH 5:30-31

You see, Jeremiah saw the destruction coming, and he said, "You like it the way you have it. You don't want change, but what will you do with what's about to unfold before you?" I'd like to pair that with a passage from Isaiah:

> *Transgressing and denying the LORD,*
> *And turning away from our God,*
> *Speaking oppression and revolt,*
> *Conceiving in and uttering from the heart lying words.*
> *Justice is turned back,*
> *And righteousness stands far away;*
> *For truth has stumbled in the street,*
> *And uprightness cannot enter.*

ISAIAH 59:13-14

If we take those two passages and try to distill them, it describes a season that is horrible and shocking from God's perspective. He's not talking about the condition of the wicked, or the ungodly, or the people with whom He doesn't have a covenant. He's talking about the attitude within the hearts of His covenant people, and it's described as horrible and shocking. I believe that's a pretty accurate description of contemporary life in American Christianity.

Then God said, "Those counted upon to tell the truth, lie. The prophets prophesy lies and the priests ignore the truth. They prefer their own authority, the authority that comes from their own power and the accumulation of their own power. Those counted upon to tell the truth, lie." I think that's a pretty accurate description, again, of our contemporary culture. Those in places we have counted on for truth-telling, even if there was a personal cost to it—an individual sacrifice—they have failed. I've been in multiple discussions in recent weeks and months with people that are responsible for decisions at all sorts of levels throughout our culture, and one message has been consistent. They say that people don't trust the messaging any longer. They don't trust the politicians. They don't trust the media. They don't know where to turn, and it's added to and fostered confusion and fear.

The prophet said that God's authority had been rejected in favor of the opinion of men.

Knowing the Word of God is one of our strongest protections against choosing the approval of people

over the authority of God. We have to determine we're
going to get to know our Bibles.

Then, the prophet said the people like it this way; they like the circumstances. They were content to let it play out, and they liked what it was bringing to them.

Much of our frustration and consternation in this season is that our routines have been disrupted. There's a lot of angst: "How do we get back to where we were? How do we get back to where we were economically? How do we get back to where we were in the school systems? How do we get back to where we were in the universities? Folks, the trajectory we were on prior to the virus was taking us towards destruction. God has intervened. He's given us a chance for some personal evaluations, some individual reflection to turn our hearts and our faces to Him. And Isaiah said, "Truth stumbles and uprightness is not welcome." It's more common than not in the public square these days to find that we mock uprightness. I'm not even certain that within the Church culture, under that general umbrella, that we've encouraged uprightness and righteousness in our children and young people. God be merciful to us.

It's not a different message in the New Testament:

Let no one in any way deceive you, for it [the return of the Lord] *will not come unless the apostasy comes first, and the man of lawlessness is revealed, the son of destruction ...*

2 THESSALONIANS 2:3

Paul's giving the Thessalonian church a window into the season that will precede our Lord's return to the earth, and he gave us some characteristics. He said, "There'll be an apostasy, a falling away, a turning from the truth."

I can tell you, as a matter of fact, that there is unprecedented apostasy in American religious life—you see it in the refusal to accept the Word of God as the authoritative rule for our faith and practice. It's apostasy to say that our ideas need to evolve, that our definitions of the family, our definitions of sexuality and human behavior shouldn't be constrained by something as antiquated as the Bible. Those aren't positions that we find just in university settings. We find them in churches, and we tolerate them in our public institutions. How can that be?

The awkward part of this discussion is that we're the most overtly Christian nation on the planet. We're the most outwardly Christian nation that remains. We're the most influential Christian nation—partially because of our wealth, partially because of our communications tools. There are several layers to that, but we have a unique responsibility. God has given us liberty and freedom and blessing and abundance so that we could take the gospel of the Kingdom to the whole world. And we've been a bit reluctant even to acknowledge the uniqueness of Jesus. We've been a little timid to say what Jesus said of Himself—that no man comes to the Father except by Him, that He is the Way, the Truth, and the Life. That's our message. Paul warns Timothy about this:

> *The Spirit clearly says that in later times some will abandon the faith and follow deceiving spirits and things taught by demons.*
>
> 1 TIMOTHY 4:1

When the truth is rejected—when we won't tolerate it in our schools, when we won't tolerate it in the Supreme Court, when we won't tolerate it in the halls of government—when we reject God's truth, demonic influences fill the void. And we begin to descend, to deteriorate into all sorts of ungodly choices and immoral behavior. We begin to establish new norms. James describes this spiritual descent:

> *But if you have bitter jealousy and selfish ambition in your heart, do not be arrogant and so lie against the truth. This wisdom is not that which comes down from above, but is earthly, natural, demonic. For where jealousy and selfish ambition exist, there is disorder and every evil thing.*
>
> JAMES 3:14-16

James is the plain language book of the New Testament. If

you're having kind of a blue day, maybe you shouldn't read James. He gets in your business. But he reminds us that carnal responses from those who "purport" to be God's people open the floodgates for disorder and every evil thing. We don't have to cast about for cause and effect. If we will humble ourselves and pray, God will move. That is such a freeing idea, if we can get our hearts around it.

III. A RESPONSE—WHAT CAN WE DO?

Now, I want to see if we can craft a response, because I'm not a pessimist. I think we're standing on the precipice of the greatest moving of the Spirit of God that we've ever known. I believe we can see the gospel of the Kingdom preached in the world with a clarity and an authority and a pervasiveness that will exceed anything our world has ever known. I believe we'll see the Spirit of God move in power and lives will be changed—people will walk out of the shadows in humility and repent, that the fear of God will come upon entire blocks of people in ways we haven't seen. I believe, in the future of our own congregation, we will see more people coming to faith, being filled with the Holy Spirit, and cooperating with God than any time in our history as a congregation. I believe it, but I don't believe it will happen in a vacuum. It will happen because of our choices, because of our willingness to bend our knee and to change our hearts.

So what can we do? What is our response to be? That's the

question I'm asked more than anything else in this season. I think we feel powerless; we feel helpless; we feel overwhelmed. Well, I want to go back to the advice of James:

> *Therefore, get rid of all moral filth and the evil that is so prevalent and humbly accept the word planted in you, which can save you. Do not merely listen to the word, and so deceive yourselves. Do what it says.*
>
> JAMES 1:21-22

Again, the language is very plain. It's clear that James isn't writing to pagans, to the ungodly, or the immoral. He's speaking to people that he imagines to be part of the Church, and he said, "Get rid of all moral filth and the evil that is so prevalent, so widespread, so easily embraced, and humbly accept God's Word that is planted in you."

If you need a little more definition—if you just casually shrug that off and say, "Well, there's no moral filth in me"—then I'll give you a little bit of a homework assignment. Go take Galatians chapter 5, verses 19 and 20, and just meditate on them. Ask the Spirit of God if you've given any place in your life to those expressions of your carnal nature. You see, I think we often think of sin as being some huge, gross, immoral act—a serial killer, or somebody who is planning acts of terrorism against large groups of people, but it's the small things. It's the things we tolerate, the attitudes of our heart, the behaviors we excuse, the obedience that we don't give expression to. It's what make us vulnerable. And James' instruction isn't to get rid of most of it, or the ones that are most troubling, but to not tolerate any: "Get rid of all the filth," he said. Don't give your carnal nature an excuse. Don't justify it. The poor behavior of someone else does not justify our equally poor behavior. We've been accepting of it for too long—not of others, but of our own selves.

We are in a battle. And there are some amazing things happening. Our own state legislature recently passed the Fetal Heartbeat Bill. It was a part of our governor's legislative agenda. It'll protect the lives of untold hundreds of children across Tennessee. It's a powerful step. There are already enormous dollars flowing into the legal suits to counteract it. But your prayers, your voice, your influence, and your awareness makes a difference.

James said to humble ourselves and accept God's Word. If you don't read it, you don't know it well enough to accept it.

Then, he said we have to choose to be obedient. Obedience is a choice. Most choices in my life that have discipline attached to them are not always attached to a sense of fun. And if I get to choose, I'd rather have cake than vegetables. If I get to choose, I'd rather have ice cream than broccoli—every time. But I've learned that for my well-being, I have to sometimes make choices that reflect discipline more than just a preference towards pleasure. The same is true in our pursuit of the Lord.

A. SARDIS, MESSAGE TO A CHURCH

I want to borrow two messages to two churches. They're delivered by Jesus, Himself. The book of Revelation opens with messages to seven churches, and I'd like to borrow the messages to two of those.

First, do you have the imagination that there are angels attached to communities of faith, that we're not just here on our own? Do you have an imagination that we're not just a glorified Bible study society, and we're not just here because of a style of worship, that there's actually angelic involvement in who we are and what we're doing? You see, we're typically more willing to believe in unclean or unhealthy spiritual forces than we are in the benefit of the angels that stand guard over us. We want to begin to align our lives with the truth of God, and listen to the Spirit of God, so that we can receive the full benefit of those forces that have been arrayed on our behalf.

In Revelation, chapter 3, is a message to the church of Sardis says:

> *"To the angel of the church in Sardis write: These are the words of him who holds the seven spirits of God and the seven stars. I know your deeds; you have a reputation of being alive, but you are dead.*
>
> *Wake up! Strengthen what remains and is about to die, for I have not found your deeds complete in the sight of my God.*
>
> *Remember, therefore, what you have received and heard; obey it, and repent. But if you do not wake up, I will come like a thief, and you will not know at what time I will come to you.*
>
> *Yet you have a few people in Sardis who have not soiled their clothes. They will walk with me, dressed in white, for they are worthy.*
>
> *He who overcomes will, like them, be dressed in white. I will never blot out his name from the book of life, but will acknowledge his name before my Father and his angels.*
>
> *He who has an ear, let him hear what the Spirit says to the churches."*
>
> REVELATION 3:1-6

It's a sobering passage. Again, it's written to believers, not the pagans or the ungodly. It's not delivered to a group of people that have devolved into pagan revelry. It's written to a church.

He says that you have a reputation, but it doesn't line up with your reality. Your reputation is that you're alive, but your reality is you're dead. Lots of activity, lots of movement, lots of things you can point to, but you're spiritually dead!

Then, He says it more plainly: "Wake up, you're asleep! Wake up!" If I had to look for one word that describes contemporary American evangelicalism, I think *asleep* would be the most accurate. It's not necessarily a description of wickedness or evil. When you're asleep, you're unconcerned, you're uninvolved. You're just unaware. Rest is a necessary thing, but if all you do is rest, you forfeit what you were created for—the productivity of your life. We've been inert long enough. When we were presented with ungodliness and immorality and wickedness, we were told that we should be tolerant, and so we were silent. Then we observed that when those who had been advocating for wickedness or ungodly immorality gained a position of authority and power, they were anything but tolerant and wanted to eliminate any dissent. We better wake up! We better stand for the truth of the Living God that He's put in our hearts.

Then Jesus said to the church at Sardis: "You need to get stronger; your deeds are incomplete." Again, I think we've got to reimagine a little bit how we've understood our faith. "Pastor, I said the Sinner's Prayer, I've been baptized, I volunteer some, I even give some." Jesus is acknowledging that they've had some momentum, but He said, "You've got to get stronger, you have things to overcome!" I think the first response that comes through is, "Well, I'm not sure I want to. Couldn't we just go back to the safer place where I could nap more?" And the answer is, "No." That's where we started with Isaiah and Jeremiah when the people said, "We like it the way it is." I believe we need to hear what the Spirit is saying to us: We're going to have to get stronger; we're going to have to train in new ways.

Then Jesus said, "You have to obey and repent." Maybe the most sobering part of that whole message is when He said, "I'll never blot out his name from the book of life, those who overcome." But He's opened the possibility of your name being blotted out. We've been a bit smug. We've been self-certain, a bit self-righteous. We'd rather reflect on the security of our position, than focus on the responsibility of our lives as Christ-followers. We don't earn our way to Heaven. That's nonsense. We could never qualify or be good enough to justify the grace and the mercy of God, but there is a responsibility that comes with being a recipient of grace.

B. LAODICEA, MESSAGE TO A CHURCH

Now, I said two churches. The other church is Laodicea. It's in the same chapter, Revelation 3, and the message is very similar. Jesus said, "I know your deeds."

Have you ever thought of that—I mean really thought about it—reflected on, spent days walking around thinking, *Jesus is paying attention to what I do*. "I know your deeds." Nothing's hidden from Him. It's not hard to fool Pastor; he's not that clever. But Jesus said, "I know your deeds."

Here's what He said to that church:

"I know your deeds, that you are neither cold nor hot. I wish you were either one or the other! So, because you are lukewarm-- neither hot nor cold--I am about to spit you out of my mouth. You say, 'I am rich; I have acquired wealth and do not need a thing.' But you do not realize that you are wretched, pitiful, poor, blind and naked. I counsel you to buy from me gold refined in the fire, so you can become rich; and white clothes to wear, so you can cover your shameful nakedness; and salve to put on your eyes, so you can see. Those whom I love I rebuke and discipline. So be earnest, and repent. Here I am! I stand at the door and knock. If anyone hears my voice and opens the door, I will come in and eat with him, and he with me."

REVELATION 3:15-20

That's an intriguing comparison to me. He said, "We say of ourselves that I'm rich and I don't need anything." But He said, "In reality, you're blind and naked." I want to ask you a question:

How deceived do you have to be to be blind and naked and not know it? This isn't a subtle thing. Jesus describes it as lukewarm. You see, I don't think we imagine that comparison is lukewarm. That feels completely frozen, but that's not how Jesus sees it. He said, "If you don't recognize that you have a need—if you're not aware of your dependence, if you imagine that you're self-sufficient, that you have acquired everything necessary for your journey—if those thoughts have taken root in your heart and your emotions," He said, "you're wretched and pitiful, blind and naked."

But then He gives us a solution. He said, "I counsel you to buy from me gold refined in the fire, so you can become rich; and white clothes to wear, so you can cover your shameful nakedness; and salve to put on your eyes, so you can see." He doesn't abandon them; He doesn't cast them out. It's not a shame-based analysis. It's an accurate diagnosis with the resolution. *You have a terminal condition and you're about to be terminated, but there's a treatment that's a hundred percent effective.* That's good news!

"Those whom I love I rebuke and discipline." May I make a suggestion? If the Spirit of God begins to bring conviction to you—if you become ill-at-ease with an attitude, with a part of your past, with a behavior, with a habit, whatever it may be— repent. A lot of times that awareness will be delivered through something somebody says to you, or through something you read. It doesn't usually just arrive in the abstract. Many times the conviction of the Spirit of God will begin when an idea is delivered to you, and the temptation is to be angry, or a bit resentful, or to do a little comparison—"Well, I'm not taking any coaching from them. They're more wicked than I am." I want to suggest a different approach. I want to take the counsel that Jesus gave us: "Those whom I love, I rebuke and I discipline." If you find that happening in your heart or your thoughts or your emotions, rather than be resentful or embittered, how about just saying quietly within yourself, "Lord, I'm listening. I'm listening. I'll accept a rebuke from a pagan. If You want to bring counsel to me from an ungodly source, I'm listening."

"Those whom I love I rebuke and I discipline. So be earnest, and repent. Here I am! I stand at the door and knock. If anyone hears my voice and opens the door, I will come in and eat with him, and he with me."

I remember that my grandmother had a picture in her home. It was Jesus standing at the door. Remember that picture? It had that verse of scripture on it. I remember reading it as a boy in her house when we would visit. I always thought of it in terms of evangelism. Jesus is standing at the door at the heart of somebody who's an unbeliever and He's knocking. And if the unbeliever would open the door and let Him come in, they could be a part of the Kingdom of God. It's a nice thought; it's just not the context. It's written to a church; it's

> written to believers—to a group of believers who were
> self-assured, so smug and so self-righteous, they're not
> aware they have any need. There's nothing desperate
> about their faith. And Jesus said they're in a position
> so desperate, they're about to forfeit everything and
> be spewed out of His mouth. And He said, "But I'm
> standing at the door asking for an invitation. And if
> you'll invite Me in, I'll come in."

What do we have to lose by saying to the Lord, "I'm sorry for my heart condition. Even though I haven't understood fully my responses and why I sat in the middle of the decay of our social society and the collapse of the influence of Christianity— I've presided over that. And I've managed to say to myself, 'It couldn't be me.' I'm sorry, Lord. I want to welcome You into my life." It's a powerful, powerful message for us.

Now, Jesus said He'd give us white clothes to wear. In Revelation 19, it's "the righteous acts of the saints." I know righteousness is a gift from Jesus, but our willingness to act righteously earns a reward from our Father in Heaven. Not to earn our way into the blessings of God, but God responds to our choices to act righteously. In Revelations 7, it's our application of the cross— the redemptive work of Jesus.

I think it's worth noting the sequence of what Jesus said to us: "Be earnest and repent." Conviction will precede repentance. I'm asking the Lord to give us some holy discontentment, to stir us a little bit, so that we won't be satisfied. If you lose some sleep, if you engage in some things that you've been fully comfortable in doing previously, I'm praying you're less comfortable with them if they don't honor the Lord fully—that any place where we've been lukewarm, that we'll begin to have a sense of discontentment. If we've put our trust in things, or ourselves, or our strength, or our wisdom, I'm asking that the Spirit of God will begin to convict us, so that we can choose the response of repentance.

So this is our target. We're going to begin to say, "God we're not asking for You to raise up somebody else. We're not asking for somebody else to be different. We're saying to You that we're going to choose You with our whole hearts like we've never chosen You before. No more excuses, and no more sloppiness. We understand the significance of the season." And I believe we'll see God respond.

If you're conscious of something you've tolerated, something you've accepted, if you would say, "Lord, I repent. I want to turn away from any expression of carnality. Lord, I'm going to choose right now to walk a new way. Lord, I was wrong. Be merciful to me." If you need to forgive, forgive. If you need forgiveness, repent of your sin and receive the forgiveness. Stop making excuses, and pray this prayer:

Heavenly Father, I come before You in humility. I have wandered from Your truth. I have become comfortable with deception and darkness, and turned my attention toward my own ambition. I have valued convenience more than obedience. Forgive me of my sins. Soften my heart once again. Open my ears to hear Your direction. Bring a spirit of conviction into my life. I lift my voice to You, for only You can bring salvation to my life. You are a faithful God—a God of mercy and truth—and I choose to yield to You with my whole heart, mind, soul and body. In Jesus' name, amen.

GOD BLESS AMERICA AGAIN

GREAT BLESSING, GREAT RESPONSIBILITY

The truth is, God has blessed our nation, over, and over, and over, and we are asking Him to bless us once again. Not because we deserve it, but because He is a God of mercy, and grace, and kindness, and He delights in showing mercy even to the wicked. We certainly don't deserve His blessings, but the underlying premise has really to do with the authority that is invested in the people of God. I am grateful for all the efforts that are being made to bring some stability and restoration to our nation, but if the Church doesn't occupy the place that we are called to be, those efforts will not succeed. We need others to do the things that they uniquely can do, but the Church has a role to play, an assignment. There is a unique authority invested in us. So we are going to take this chapter to look at the great blessings that God has shown us and the great responsibility that comes with that.

I. HISTORY MATTERS IN THE PRESENT

I want to start with just a bit of history, because I think we live in a very unique nation—the greatest nation on the face of the earth. Now, God loves people from every nation, race, language, and tribe. Having said that; however, I believe the United States is a unique representation of the grace and mercy of God. We are unique amongst the nations of the world—both in our history and our founding documents—and in the mission of faith from which our nation was birthed. It doesn't mean that we are perfect or that our history is perfect. I am not suggesting that. But sometimes, in our complaints and bitterness about our own nation, we reflect quite an ignorance of the nations of the world.

I suspect you have heard of the United States Declaration of Independence. The Preamble to that document says this:

> *"We hold these truths to be self-evident, that all men are created equal, that they are endowed by their Creator with certain unalienable Rights, that among these are Life, Liberty and the pursuit of Happiness."* *

The authors of the Declaration of Independence reveal in our founding documents that they believed in a Creator of Heaven and Earth. And when they were giving shape to this nation

---

* *United States of America Declaration of Independence (US 1776)*

that we enjoy today, they did it understanding that we lived under the authority of that Creator of Heaven and Earth. The Preamble is somewhat familiar, but less so is the conclusion of that document:

> *"We, therefore, the Representatives of the United States of America, in General Congress, Assembled, appealing to the Supreme Judge of the world for the rectitude of our intentions, do, in the Name, and by the Authority of the good People of these Colonies, solemnly publish and declare, That these United Colonies are, and of Right ought to be, Free and Independent States; ... And for the support of this Declaration, with a firm reliance on the protection of divine Providence, we mutually pledge to each other our Lives, our Fortunes and our sacred Honor."* **

Again, the document that declared our independence as a nation was rooted in the awareness and the knowledge of dependence upon a living God to allow our nation to be birthed. When the Constitution was drafted, the founders—the drafters—recognized that it would not be passed. It wouldn't be ratified by the colonies or the newly acknowledged states unless they attached to it a Bill of Rights for the citizens of our nation. The first Ten Amendments of our Constitution are the rights of the people in this nation. They are not the rights of the

---

** *United States of America Declaration of Independence (US 1776)*

government. In fact, the concern of the framers when they put our Constitution together was that government would assume the power and authority that was intended for the people to have.

The very first Amendment, and not first simply in number, I believe, was first in priority. You may know a portion of it:

> *"Congress shall make no law respecting an establishment of religion, or prohibiting the free exercise thereof; or abridging the freedom of speech, or of the press; or the right of the people peaceably to assemble, and to petition the government for a redress of grievances."* *

Did you see that? The very first Amendment of our Constitution says that Congress can make no law that would in any way prohibit the free exercise of our religion, abridge the freedom of speech, or the press, or prohibit the right of the people to peaceably assemble, or petition the government for a redress of grievances.

There wasn't anything like it in the world when it was first put to paper, or even today. It reflects a wisdom that went beyond the capabilities of the individuals who contributed to it. It is fashionable these days to be angry at our nation, and there are

---

* *United States of America Constitution Amendment I (US 1791)*

reasons to be angry. I am not even trying to deny that, but I am telling you that to have a disproportional hatred for our nation and our history reflects a lack of awareness of the history of the nations of the world, and we don't have to go back into antiquity to see that. Let's look at some of the leading nations in our current season.

You know it is very popular in the Olympics to celebrate the nations and cultures of the world. When the Olympics visit other nations or when we watch the Olympics—when they are not interrupted by viruses—it is common for us to celebrate the great civilizations and nations of the world, and that is not inappropriate. People of every nation, race, language, and tribe make up the Church of Jesus Christ. But not every nation is founded with the liberties, freedoms, and opportunities that we know. Even today, we are unique in the world. And our history, as sketchy as it may be, is unique in the world.

Russia, have you heard of them? Joseph Stalin, one of their pivotal leaders of the last century, was responsible for 20,000,000 Russians losing their lives—20,000,000 people. We don't hear a lot about that when we celebrate the strength of that nation.

We have been told almost unrelentingly now for two or three decades about how tremendous the culture and the history of China are. The Chinese people are children of God, created in His image, just as we are. I am not saying that the people in any way are devalued, but the political structure that overarches them holds them in a very oppressed space. Mao Tse-Tung, I suspect you've heard of him, initiated a reform movement in China. He called it the "Great Leap Forward," and in a four-year window it resulted in 45,000,000 deaths in China. Can you imagine that? In a four-year window, 45,000,000 people lost their lives because of the decisions and the policies of a leader. In more contemporary history, they've enforced a two-child policy, forced abortion, and female infanticide—resulting in about 15,000,000 abortions annually in China. Again, this is not an indictment of the people, but the system under which they live is cruel and oppressive.

Islam occupies a large part of our globe. In those places where Islam is the predominant political and religious authority over the people in those nations, it serves as an oppressive force. I spent a good deal of time in the Middle East. You take Lebanon, Syria, Iraq, Iran, Egypt, Sudan, Yemen, and North Africa—across those nations it's very difficult to argue that women are treated in any way as equal. Outsiders—if you're not a Muslim, you are subjected to a Dhimmi tax—economic servitude. They are not nations of equal opportunity.

Now, in our current world, if you dare to remind anyone of these ideas or these principles in a public place you're shouted down as xenophobic—that you don't like people from other countries. Nothing could be further from the truth. My heart's desire is to see people from every nation, from every language, from every people group, know the lordship of Jesus of Nazareth in their lives. He'll bring freedom to them, opportunity to them, and deliverance to them—with understanding that we stand equal at the foot of the cross. We're told these days that if we advocate for a biblical view of family and human sexuality that it's hate speech, or perhaps that you're homophobic. Well, folks, the reality—whether it's acknowledged in those public places or not—is that Christianity is the hope of humanity. Jesus changes us from the inside out.

The American Church has an enormous opportunity. We have greater liberties, freedoms, and protections under our legal system to be advocates for Jesus of Nazareth than in almost any nation on the planet. And up until very recently, we have taken that as a significant assignment—a responsibility, a mission—of our nation. But in recent years, we have been bullied a bit. We've said that the proclamation of the gospel and the uniqueness of Jesus are somehow inappropriate. In fact, it's become quite popular from the highest offices of our nation even, to assert that we're not a Christian nation. We've even had United States presidents echo that sentiment. Now, it's true that we're not a theocracy. We never have been. It's equally true that we are tolerant of other faiths. No matter what faith you choose and how you choose to worship, you're entitled to equal treatment under our law, and should be. It's true that we're an inclusive society, and we'll embrace diversity of beliefs and do our best to live with one another respectfully. It's true that our founders clearly did not want a State Church to be founded so that the government dictated theology. However, we are unmistakably a nation with a Christian heritage, and I would submit to you that as Christ-followers we have the same right to celebrate that heritage as enthusiastically, as intentionally, and as boisterously as any other group has a right to celebrate their heritage in this nation.

It is true that those pioneering in founding this nation sought freedom to worship the God of Abraham, Isaac, and Jacob. The Mayflower Compact was the first governing document of the Plymouth Colony. It was written by the Separatists, who would later be known as the Pilgrims who crossed the Atlantic aboard the Mayflower, seeking freedom to practice Christianity according to their own determination, and not according to the will of the English Church. It was signed on November 11, 1620, by more than 41 of the ship's passengers. You may or may not know that our finest universities, our most celebrated universities, were begun as schools to train Christian ministers.

Harvard University, the oldest institution of higher learning in the United States, was founded 16 years after the arrival of the Pilgrims at Plymouth. Harvard College was established in 1636, by a vote of the Great and General Court of the Massachusetts Bay Colony. It was named for its first benefactor, John Harvard, of Charleston. He was a young minister, who upon his death in 1638, left his library and half his estate to the new institution. Princeton University received its first charter from King George II, under the seal of John Hamilton, the acting Governor of the

Royal Province of New Jersey, on October 22, 1746.

Princeton is the fourth college to be established in the British Colonies after Harvard, William and Mary, and Yale. It was the first in the Middle Colonies. The Charter was obtained through the efforts of a number of Presbyterians, under the direct influence of the Great Awakening. If you're not familiar with it, it was a religious revival that swept the Colonies in the early eighteenth century, the 1700's. Six of Princeton's seven original Trustees were graduates of Yale, who believed Yale no longer provided a suitable atmosphere in which men could be trained for truly enlightened pulpits.

It's true that the individuals who founded our nation were overwhelmingly Christian men, and understood their actions to be guided by God. It's true that our founding documents— the Constitution and the Bill of Rights—reflect a value system clearly derived from Scripture. In Washington, D.C., our Supreme Court Building, the Halls of Congress, and many other D.C. buildings, which house significant government functions, have scriptures prominently carved into the stone with which they're erected.

The liberty and freedom we know today has emerged from a Christian worldview. Ideas like equality before the law, women's rights, children's rights, fair labor practices, tolerance, and civil rights—all of those have emerged from a Judeo-Christian worldview. We act as if all of the world knows the liberties and freedoms that we do, and this simply isn't true. We are unique. The liberties, freedoms, and opportunities we have, have come to us as an inheritance, and are not to be rested upon and gobbled up as we stamp our feet like petulant children, demanding the government provide something else for us. They are a heritage to be protected, guarded, and extended to one another, and handed down to the generation who follows us.

Did you know that 52 of the 55 signers of the Declaration of Independence were orthodox, deeply committed Christians? The other three all believed in the Bible as divine truth, and in the God of Scripture and in His personal intervention in history. It's the same Congress that formed the American Bible Society. Immediately after creating the Declaration of Independence, the Continental Congress voted to purchase and import 20,000 copies of Scripture for the people of this nation.

Patrick Henry, who is often called the firebrand of the American Revolution, is still remembered for his words, "Give me liberty, or give me death." In the current textbooks, the context of those words has been deleted. Here is the rest of what he said:

> "An appeal to arms and the God of hosts is all that is left to us. But we shall not fight our battles alone. There is a just God who presides over the destinies of nations. The battle, sir, is not to the strong alone. Is life so dear, or peace so sweet, as to be purchased at the price of chains and slavery? Forbid it, Almighty God! I know not what course others may take; but

as for me, give me liberty or give me death!" *

PATRICK HENRY, MARCH 23, 1775

I wonder what would happen if the Church in the twenty-first century recognized that Almighty God had given us an assignment. What if we attached a value of significance to it that somewhat reflected the values that our founding generation attached to the assignment they understood God had given to them? Now those sentences have been erased from our textbooks long ago. Was Patrick Henry a Christian? Well, in his Last Will and Testament, he wrote this:

> *"This is all the Inheritance I can give to my dear family, The religion of Christ can give them one which will make them rich indeed."* **

PATRICK HENRY, 1798

Consider the words of George Washington, in his farewell speech on September 19, 1796:

> *"Of all the dispositions and habits that lead to political prosperity, our religion and morality are the indispensable supporters ... And let us with caution indulge the supposition that morality can be maintained without religion ... Reason*

----

* *Patrick Henry, Give Me Liberty or Give Me Death (1775)*

** *Patrick Henry, Last Will and Testament (1798)*

and experience both forbid us to expect that our national morality can prevail in exclusion of religious principles."

GEORGE WASHINGTON, 1796

It was 1782 when the United States Congress voted a resolution in which they "recommend this edition of the Bible to the inhabitants of the United States."

Of the first 108 universities founded in America, 106 were distinctly Christian. As I mentioned, that included the first Harvard, chartered in 1636. In the original Harvard Student Handbook, Rule Number One was that students seeking entrance must know Latin and Greek so that they could study the Scriptures. You might not know that for over 100 years, more than 50 percent of all Harvard graduates were pastors.

It's clear from history that the Bible and the Christian faith were foundational to our educational and judicial system. However, in about 1947, there was a radical change in the direction of our Supreme Court. It required ignoring every precedent of Supreme Court ruling for the previous 160 years. The Supreme Court ruled in a limited way to affirm a wall of separation between Church and State in the public classroom. In the coming years, this led to removing prayer from the public schools. That was 1962. Do you happen to know the prayer that caused so much furor it was banished by our Supreme Court?

------

* *George Washington, George Washington's Farewell Speech (1796)*

This is it: "Almighty God, we acknowledge our dependence on Thee. We beg Your blessings upon us, and our parents, and our teachers, and our country. Amen." That was deemed inappropriate, and we said little. In 1963, the Supreme Court ruled that Bible reading was outlawed as unconstitutional in the public school system. The Court offered this justification: "If portions of the New Testament were read without explanation, they could and have been psychologically harmful to children." Bible reading was now unconstitutional, though the Bible had been frequently quoted by those who wrote our Constitution and shaped our nation and its systems of education, justice, and government.

In 1965, the Courts denied as unconstitutional the right of a student at a public cafeteria to bow his head and pray audibly for his food. In 1980, Stone v. Graham outlawed the Ten Commandments in our public schools. The Supreme Court said this: "If the posted copies of the Ten Commandments were to have any effect at all, it would be to induce school children to read them, and if they read them and meditated upon them, and perhaps venerated and obeyed them, this is not a permissible objective." Is it not a permissible objective to allow our children to follow the moral principles of the Ten Commandments? James Madison, the primary author of the Constitution of the United States, said this:

"The belief in a God All-Powerful, wise, and good is so

essential to the moral order of the world and to the happiness of man that arguments which enforce it cannot be drawn from too many sources nor adapted with too much solicitude to the different characters and capacities to be impressed with it." [*]

JAMES MADISON

II. EACH GENERATION MUST CHOOSE TO HONOR GOD

Now, we would have never allowed the Ten Commandments to be taken down in the schools if we had held them in high esteem in our homes. Today, we ask God to bless America, but how can He bless a nation that has departed from Him? Revisionists have rewritten history to remove the truth about our country's Christian heritage. It's not lost. We still have breath. The Church is still present. We can still gather, and I believe with all of my heart that if we will humble ourselves and seek God, and turn from our sins, He will bring healing to our nation (2 Chronicles 7:14), because that's true to His character in spite of the failures and flaws of our own. Each generation has to choose to honor God—each generation. We have a tremendous heritage, but that is not enough. We have to choose God for ourselves in the twenty-first century.

---

[*] *James Madison, Letter to Frederick Beasley (1825)*

I want to look at a passage from Ezekiel. Ezekiel is an interesting character in Scripture. He lives in Babylon, but it says that God took him by a lock of his hair and took him to Jerusalem to show him what was happening in the city. That's an exciting prayer life. I want to read you portions from Ezekiel, chapters 8 and 9. God takes him to the sanctuary, the Temple in Jerusalem, and shows him what is happening there. He wants Ezekiel to see the abominations that are being performed—not in some dark corner, but in the Temple in Jerusalem. Now, remember this is the covenant people of God, living in the land that He has promised to them, worshipping in a temple that was dedicated to the God of Abraham, Isaac, and Jacob:

And He said to me, "Go in and see the wicked abominations that they are committing here." So I entered and looked, and behold, every form of creeping things and beasts and detestable things, with all the idols of the house of Israel, were carved on the wall all around. Standing in front of them were seventy elders of the house of Israel, with Jaazaniah the son of Shaphan standing among them, each man with his censer in his hand and the fragrance of the cloud of incense (worship) rising. Then He said to me, "Son of man, do you see what the elders of the house of Israel are committing in the dark, each man in the room of his carved images? For they say, 'The LORD does not see us; the LORD has forsaken the land.'" And He said to me, "Yet you will see still greater abominations which they are committing."

Then He brought me to the entrance of the gate of the LORD'S house which was toward the north; and behold, women were sitting there weeping for Tammuz. He said to me, "Do you see this, son of man? Yet you will see still greater abominations than these."

Then He brought me into the inner court of the LORD'S house. And behold, at the entrance to the temple of the LORD, between the porch and the altar, were about twenty-five men with their backs to the temple of the LORD and their faces toward the east; and they were prostrating themselves eastward toward the sun. He said to me, "Do you see this, son of man? Is it too light a thing for the house of Judah to commit the abominations which they have committed here, that they have filled the land with violence and provoked Me repeatedly? "Therefore, I indeed will deal in wrath. My eye will have no pity nor will I spare; and though they cry in My ears with a loud voice, yet I will not listen to them."

EZEKIEL 8:9-18

I know it's a longer passage, but there were 70 elders worshipping idols in the Temple of God. God said, "It was an abomination." Now, there was a group of women gathered to worship a Canaanite pagan fertility god, and another group of men had turned their backs on the Temple and were worshipping the Sun. And God said to Ezekiel, "I'll bring my judgment upon these people, My Covenant people. In spite of all the miracles and the deliverance that is a part of their story, in spite of My Temple in the midst of this city, I'll step into history and bring judgment."

Then Ezekiel continues:

> *Then He cried out in my hearing with a loud voice saying, "Draw near, O executioners of the city, each with his destroying weapon in his hand." Behold, six men came from the direction of the upper gate which faces north, each with his shattering weapon in his hand; and among them was a certain man clothed in linen with a writing case at his loins. And they went in and stood beside the bronze altar.*
>
> *Then the glory of the God of Israel went up from the cherub on which it had been, to the threshold of the temple. And He called to the man clothed in linen at whose loins was the writing case. The LORD said to him, "Go through the midst of the city, even through the midst of Jerusalem, and put a mark on the foreheads of the men who sigh and groan over all the abominations which are being committed in its midst." But to the others He said in my hearing, "Go through the city after him and strike; do not let your eye have pity and do not spare. Utterly slay old men, young men, maidens, little children, and women, but do not touch any man on whom is the mark; and you shall start from My sanctuary." So they started with the elders who were before the temple.*

EZEKIEL 9:1-6

55

Judgment began in Jerusalem at the House of God, and in God's economy, judgment begins at the House of God. I believe those passages are relevant to contemporary American history. In fact, I think they're relevant to the whole Western world. The professing Church has been infiltrated by a spiritual filth and wickedness that is unprecedented in the history of our nation. There is unapologetic gloating and boasting about the diminishment of the Word of God, the uniqueness of Jesus— His divinity, His redemptive work, His physical death on a cross, His bodily resurrection from the dead, His ascension to Heaven. Those concepts are mocked in some of the most celebrated institutions of Christian training. They're not welcome in many of the pulpits any longer. Notions of sin, and morality, and immorality aren't welcomed in too many of our places of worship.

Some of you are old enough to remember the rebellion of the 1960's. Folks, the rebellion that we saw in the streets of the 60's hasn't stopped. It's just become more respectable. It's infiltrated the corridors of power, government, academia, even the Church. Immorality is the new morality. We're told that morality these days is based on personal preference. God hasn't changed His mind. In fact, there is an entirely new wave of Scripture exegesis, in interpreting Scripture that is taught in the most celebrated theology schools in our nation. It's not a new thing. It has been in place for a season, but biblical texts are declared hopelessly patriarchal, and *patriarchal* is a toxic term. They reject the notion almost entirely, saying it celebrates the domination of men over innocent women. They suggest counter readings to Scripture, alternative readings, where the text is read defiantly against the grain.

And know this—the root, the objective of all of this defiant reading of Scripture is to take those first three chapters of Genesis and set them aside, because if you can do away with those first chapters, the rest of the story unravels quickly.

I read one analysis that suggested the serpent was the liberator—that Eve was the heroine and the Lord God was a jealous tyrant who was concerned only with the preservation of His prerogatives. From that vantage point, God is cast in the role of Satan, and Satan in the role of God. And this isn't something quietly done in some hidden corner, in some dark place. This is common in the most celebrated theological institutions in our nation, the places that are training the people that are occupying pulpits and leading our churches.

Did you see who Ezekiel said would be the only group that was spared when God's judgment began? It was in chapter 9: "Put a mark on the foreheads of the men and women who sigh and groan over all the abominations which are being committed." It was only those who sighed and groaned, who grieved over what was happening. It means indifference is insufficient. Being busy with our own life plans and not paying attention won't protect us. We have to care enough about the things of God, being committed enough to seeing them extended to the generations who follow us, that we sigh and moan in grief when we see God being diminished. It's an assignment. Our prayers do matter. The thoughts and attitudes of our heart do matter.

I want to read you a verse from Amos. He's a prophet that preceded Ezekiel a bit. The word *Amos* in Hebrew means "a burden," so the book of Amos is about a man with a burden, and he's describing a group of God's people who are actually living life pretty well:

"Do you put off the day of calamity,
And would you bring near the seat of violence?

Those who recline on beds of ivory
And sprawl on their couches,
And eat lambs from the flock
And calves from the midst of the stall,

Who improvise to the sound of the harp,
And like David have composed songs for themselves,

Who drink wine from sacrificial bowls
While they anoint themselves with the finest of oils,
Yet they have not grieved over the ruin of Joseph.

Therefore, they will now go into exile at the head of
the exiles,
And the sprawlers' banqueting will pass away."

AMOS 6:3-7

Did you hear what Amos said? The same thing that Ezekiel said to us. God said, "You haven't grieved over my diminishment. You thought your affluence and your comfortable lifestyles would protect you." I believe the greatest challenge of this generation is love of self. We've allowed it to eclipse almost everything else. There is very little grief, even amongst the people of God for the ungodliness around us.

III. INTERCESSORS—SPIRIT OF ELIJAH TO CONFRONT THE SPIRIT OF JEZEBEL

So what are we to do? How do we respond? It's not enough to paint a sobering picture. We need to understand our response so that God might look upon us in mercy and grace.

A. GOD HAD SOMEONE TO STAND ...

All throughout the history of God's people, He raises up intercessors. He looks for men and women, the scripture says, who have a heart towards Him, who are willing to lay aside their own personal agenda and take up the purposes of God uniquely in that generation. The wickedest of all the Israelite kings was Ahab and his wife was Jezebel, a Phoenician that Ahab married. In all of the history of Israel, they are the gold standard for wickedness, immorality, murder and violence. But in the days of Ahab and Jezebel, God raised up Elijah, a prophet, and the spirit of Elijah stood in confrontation to what Ahab and Jezebel would do to the nation. You may know the story. Elijah called the prophets of Baal to Mount Carmel, and he called down fire from Heaven, putting to death hundreds of false prophets on the mountain that day. Then Jezebel murderously threatened:

> *Ahab told Jezebel all that Elijah had done, and how he had killed all the prophets with the sword. Then Jezebel sent a messenger to Elijah, saying, "So may the gods do to me and even more, if I do not make your life as the life of one of them by tomorrow about this time." And he was afraid and arose and ran for his life and came to Beersheba, which belongs to Judah, and left his servant there.*

1 KINGS 19:1-3

Elijah ran for his life, but God had the last word: "Of Jezebel also has the Lord spoken, saying, 'The dogs will eat Jezebel in the district of Jezreel'" (1 Kings 21:23). And they did!

In Matthew 11, Jesus attributed to John the Baptist the spirit of Elijah—someone who had come before John to prepare Israel for the message of the good news of the arrival of the Kingdom of God: "'And if you are willing to accept it, John himself is Elijah who was to come.'" The hopeful tone of Scripture is that God prepared John the Baptist to precede Jesus' ministry:

> *"And he will turn many of the sons of Israel back to the Lord their God. It is he who will go as a forerunner before Him in the spirit and power of Elijah, TO TURN THE HEARTS OF THE FATHERS BACK TO THE CHILDREN, and the disobedient to the attitude of the righteous, so as to make ready a people prepared for the Lord."*
>
> LUKE 1:16-17

God prepared Moses to stand and confront Pharaoh, and He prepared Joshua to defeat the Canaanites. He prepared Daniel to face the Babylonians and the Persians. He prepared Nehemiah to rebuild the walls of Jerusalem, and He prepared Zerubbabel to rebuild the Second Temple. God prepared Peter for Pentecost and for the Jerusalem Church, then for Cornelius and the Gentile expansion of the Jesus-story. God prepared Paul with a message for the Roman world, and I believe God has prepared a people for the twenty-first century to be advocates for Jesus of Nazareth—to stand for the truth of the gospel, not to hide in our churches—and God will provide the strength for the challenge.

B. GOD WILL PROVIDE THE STRENGTH FOR THE CHALLENGE

In Psalm 71, the psalmist declares:

> *"I will go in the strength of the Lord GOD; I will make mention of Your righteousness, of Yours only"*

PSALM 71:16

We don't go in our strength, or our wisdom, or our ability, or our resources. We stand in the strength of the Creator of Heaven and Earth. It's important to know, because the things that reign against us are intimidating, they're threatening, they're unrelenting, and they're motivated by evil. I've said on many occasions lately that I believe we're in a battle for the heart and soul of our nation, and that it is not going to be resolved by the medical community, or the health care professionals, or the legal community. It's not going to be resolved by politicians, or political parties, or elections. All of those things have a role and a place, but the Church has a unique responsibility. We're salt and light. If darkness overwhelms our nation, it's not because of immorality in the political realm. It's because of immorality in the Church.

The problems we're facing aren't somebody else's problems. They're ours. What I want to ask you to do is to begin to soberly, quietly, and consistently, say to God, "Is there anything in my heart, anything in my life that separates me from Your best? Have I glossed over my past? Have I treated my ungodliness, and my immorality, and my brokenness casually and said, 'It's insignificant'?"

If you say, "Pastor, I know for certain I need to repent. I've hidden in the church. I sat there and I've been quiet, and I didn't call any attention to myself, but I haven't really honored the Lord." If you know you need to repent, just kneel wherever you are. Take a minute before the Lord, and say this prayer:

Heavenly Father, forgive me for ignoring Your counsel and choosing my own way. I have turned my back on Your goodness and Your abundant blessings. I have chosen pride and indulgence over righteousness and purity. I humble myself today in repentance, asking for mercy. We are a nation in need of healing. Only Almighty God can restore our fortunes. I cry out to You today for mercy. I do not blame others for my circumstances; I have walked this path. This day, I acknowledge You, Almighty God as the Judge of all the earth. May the name of Jesus of Nazareth be lifted up in our homes, our city, our state, and our nation. In Jesus' name, amen.

GOD BLESS AMERICA AGAIN

THE LOVE OF TRUTH

I've suggested to you that God has uniquely blessed this nation with affluence, prosperity, liberty, and freedom. We have enjoyed the blessings of Almighty God in a very unique way. If you just casually review modern human history, you will see that the freedoms, abundance, and liberties we have enjoyed cannot be understood in any way other than having come from the hand of God. It seems to me that any other explanation falls short and is filled with enormous hubris. We truly are "one nation under God." What makes it more remarkable is that we are not a single ethnicity. We have come from all the nations of the world. Often we have been driven out, usually unwanted by our nations, or we left because of very meager opportunities. So, we came to this nation, typically with very little, but then with the blessing of God and with the gift of freedom and liberty, we have experienced abundance and opportunities for ourselves and our children that are unparalleled on planet Earth today. That's not just me pounding my chest filled with pride and American exceptionalism. Let me be clear: God is not an American. He does not love us uniquely, and I'm quite convinced that if the Church in America isn't awakened, and we don't respond with an attitude of humility and repentance, that we will see the judgment of God. It's unimaginable to me that there could be a different future. I think perhaps we still have an opportunity. I'm not even certain of that. But I know that we have lived for decades now imagining ourselves to be invincible, and it's a myth; its deception. We have flaunted the goodness of God. In our pride and our arrogance, we have taken the grace of God and mercy of God and we have chosen wickedness, immorality, selfishness, and greed. I'm not talking about beyond the Church. I'm talking about within the Church. We have treated the goodness of God in a very casual way. We have been consumed with comfort and convenience, but it's not a unique story in history. The people of God have often walked away from Him in the midst of His blessing. The beauty of the invitation of Scripture is that if we will humble ourselves and repent, God will be merciful to us. We have seen some displays of arrogance that are stunning to me, and the response of the Church has been underwhelming at best. It's the truth.

The objective in this sermon is to highlight the significance of the love of truth. If that's all you take away, I will trust that that's God's message. In 2 Thessalonians, it warns:

> *The coming of the lawless one will be in accordance with work of Satan displayed in counterfeit miracles, signs and*

wonders and in every sort of evil that deceives those who are
perishing. They perish because they refuse to love the truth
and so be saved.

2 THESSALONIANS 2:9-10

This is a description of the Antichrist emerging on to the scene of human history. We'll talk a bit more about that in a moment, but there's language there that I think is helpful. There will be an open and broad display of something that is counterfeit and yet supernatural. Not everything that is supernatural is authentic. We'll need to know the difference. It seems to me that the critical component of that admonition is that we refuse to love the truth, and in so doing, we have opened ourselves to deception. So, if I had to look for an essential component to protect us against deception, it would be the love of the truth—not a casual acquaintance with it.

When the Bible talks about the truth, it talks about it in more than one way. It refers to Jesus being the truth; the Word of God being the truth; and the Holy Spirit being the truth. We'll have to have a love for the Word of God, for Jesus and His redemptive work, and towards the Person of the Holy Spirit. We'll need more than a casual reading of our Bible and more than an occasional reading of our Bible. We'll have to be more interested in knowing what the Word of God says than our favorite programming, our favorite sports teams, or our favorite distractions. Now, I'm not against television, or sports teams, or distractions, but I think it's a vain imagination that you could treat God as a casual intrusion into your life and give your heart and your energy to those other things and imagine yourself prepared to not be deceived. We will gladly sit in the weather to watch our favorite teams play, particularly if we think it's a year when they are on the ascendancy. Now, I'm not saying that's wrong. I've done it myself. I've gone to Titans' games when it was so cold even the animals had enough sense to stay indoors, and there I sat on an aluminum bench. I know I was raised better than that. We are pretty casual when it comes to the things of God, so let's not look anyplace else right now. Let's let this be about our own selves. Don't make notes of those you wish could have a copy, and don't doodle in the margins the names of people you think need to change, or the candidates who are up for election that are dooming us to something. Let's make this about ourselves. We have treated the things of God with such a casual nature.

Now, that's our story, and we have to learn to love the truth. It's not something we do, and it's more of a marathon than a sprint. Begin to make some subtle adjustments in your behavior patterns. Begin to gradually shift the time and energy you spend on distractions and entertainment and begin to invest some of those things in prayer and reading your Bible and being with godly people. Don't give your discretionary time to people who destroy your faith. We all have people in our spheres of influence that don't know the Lord. It's a healthy thing; it's an important thing. I want those people around the periphery of my life, but the heart of my life and the heart of my discretionary time I need to spend with people who strengthen my faith. It's difficult enough for me maintain it as it is without inviting people into the core of my life who tear at it, who bring discouragement and despair. We have enough of those people involuntarily in our lives, true?

Jesus gave us some advice on how to prepare. Matthew, chapter 24, is His lengthy discourse on the end of the age and His return to earth. We are not going to unpack it, but I did bring you a sampling, because I think the single most consistent warning in that passage is a warning against deception. You know enough about biblical interpretation by now—if Jesus warns you against deception, there is a high degree of probability that we are either already deceived or we are extraordinarily vulnerable:

> *Jesus answered: "Watch out that no one deceives you. For many will come in my name, claiming, 'I am the Christ,' and will deceive many* [not a few]... *At that time many will turn away from the faith and will betray and hate each other, and many false prophets will appear and deceive many people."*
>
> MATTHEW 24:4-5, 10-11

The language suggests large numbers, big blocks of people, succumbing to deception and believing things that are false.

Remember, deception is you believing something to be true that is in reality false. It's not a message to the pagans—to the ungodly, to the people on the periphery. It's a message to people imagining themselves secure in their faith. So, if I were going to look for a single characteristic as we approach the culmination of the age, it's going to be widespread deception. Now, there will be things that will support that. There will be a turning away from the truth, an apostasy. There's unprecedented apostasy in the American Church, in an unimaginable way. At the highest levels of organizations—from the finest and most celebrated seminaries to the wealthiest and most established churches in our history as a people—we have turned away from the fundamental principles of orthodox Christianity. They are mocked in the places where we train our people to do ministry. It's not a new thing. It's been in place for decades, long enough now that it has spread its way across our country. From that apostasy comes deception. We sit in our churches, and the Word of God is not held in high esteem. The divinity of Christ isn't celebrated. The redemptive work of Jesus is looked at askew and askance as if the virgin birth is perhaps something to be debated or a naïve concept from an earlier generation. It's deception, and we need the courage to say what it is. It's very clear from the prophetic scriptures that as we approach the end of the age that there will be a true Church and a false church—and you and I need to be prepared to know the difference. If we aren't prepared to know the difference, we're deceived.

Let's take just a moment with this notion of how deception displaces truth:

> *But I am afraid that just as Eve was deceived by the serpent's cunning, your minds may somehow be led astray from your sincere and pure devotion to Christ.*

2 CORINTHIANS 11: 3

That's a startling statement to me. Paul is writing with an expression of concern to a group of believers in the Corinthian church, saying, "I'm afraid that your minds may somehow be led astray. For if someone comes to you and preaches a Jesus other than the Jesus we preached, or if you received a different spirit from the one you received, or a different gospel from the one you accepted, you put up with it easily enough." Paul is not suggesting they might be led astray from a place of carnality or wickedness; he recognizes their faith is sincere and of pure devotion to Christ. This is a far more real adversary, I believe, than we have been willing to acknowledge.

There's a challenge in the church in Corinth. The church was birthed though Paul's ministry—through his suffering and his investment in them—and a group of people have arrived in Corinth with a Jesus-story, and a gospel message, claiming to have a higher revelation. Paul refers to them as super apostles; they have a hyper faith, a deeper revelation, and greater insight. So, Paul writes to the church in Corinth, and he says, "I'm concerned for you, because you very easily put up with a different gospel. Oh, it has Jesus in the story, but it addresses your carnal nature."

If I look for one way to characterize the Corinthian church, it was a very carnal church. They struggled with immorality and drunkenness and all sorts of expressions of the works of the flesh, and Paul said, "You very easily put up with a different gospel." When we think of deception, I don't imagine deception as coming from the pagan society. Deception will emerge from the midst of the church. They'll be using church language, Jesus-language, and religious expressions, but they'll invite you towards a carnal faith, an earthly faith.

The call to be a Christ-follower is the call to lay down our lives. Jesus said, "No man can be my disciple unless you take up your cross daily and follow Me." We don't just take up the cross when we make a profession of faith. It's a lifestyle of saying no to our carnal, earthly self, and saying yes to the Spirit of God as we grow up in the Lord. If we refuse that pathway, we are highly susceptible to deception, and will embrace a form of the gospel. In 2 Timothy, chapter 3, Paul says that they'll have a form of godliness, but they're going to deny the power of it. The power of the gospel in Paul's thought is the cross. "You put up with it easily enough," he said. We have to guard our hearts, folks.

In American Christendom, we have church shopped like we restaurant shop. We have a favorite restaurant for a season—

the menu suits us, we get to know the servers, and we frequent it. Then, there is something new, or better, or different, and we shift rather casually based on absurd things, like expressions of worship. We have treated the Body of Christ and our place in the Body of Christ with extraordinary casualness, and it's affected not only the Church, but our whole culture. We watch it in professional athletics. When I was a boy, the athletes invested their lives in causing their teams to be winners. That's not the pattern any longer. They migrate, and they find the best athletes and gather together on a team, so that they can declare themselves the best. I don't think it's fair to blame it on the millennials. I think the millennial attitude emerged from the hearts and the values of those who have preceded them. We see it in every level of our culture now, and we see it in the Church. We treat it so casually. If it doesn't suit us, we withdraw. If there's an idea in a message that leaves us frustrated, we withdraw, as if withdrawing somehow puts us in a stronger or healthier place. We have to love the truth, and we can't afford to "easily enough" embrace another gospel or another idea because it feeds our own carnal selfish nature.

This leads me to some of the things that displace the truth: Deception and pride go together. When we allow ourselves to be led by our flesh, by our carnal self, as born again, Spirit-filled Christ followers, it makes us vulnerable to deception.

You can pray in the Spirit and still be a very carnal Christian. Baptism in the Holy Spirit is not evidence of maturity. It's a gift. We give gifts to the smallest of children. We give children gifts that they don't know how to embrace, understand, or operate because it gives joy to the one giving the gift, and it gives God joy to give His gifts to His children. But it's a mistake for us to interpret those gifts as expressions of maturity in our lives. Maturity is about the formation of the character of Christ in us, and that is worked out over time. That's not about the supernatural.

In Jeremiah, chapter 49, verse 16, the prophet warns: "The terror you inspire and the pride of your heart have deceived you." So, the pride in your heart makes you vulnerable to deception. It was pride that caused Satan, arguably the most remarkable of all the archangels, to forfeit his place in God's eternal purposes. It's a powerful thing. We have a little idiom that says, "Pride goes before the fall." That's not what the scripture says. It says that pride precedes "destruction." We can't afford to tolerate it.

A New Testament verse clearly states the origin of pride:

For everything in the world--the cravings of sinful man, the lust of his eyes and the boasting of what he has and does-- comes not from the Father but from the world.

1 JOHN 2:16

That's the New International Version®. The New American Standard Bible® is a bit more literal. Instead of "the boasting of what he has and what he does," it says "the pride of life." It says that the pride of what we've done and what we have accumulated doesn't come from the Father, and it opens our heart to destructive things. It's a very sober warning. Don't treat pride casually. What's the antidote to pride? Humility. Humility is acquired indirectly. You don't acquire humility in a direct way. You acquire humility by being willing to serve others. You acquire humility in a variety of ways. Take time to invite the Holy Spirit to help you review your behaviors and your attitudes. Are you engaged in behavior that will allow humility to flourish in your life? If not, you're vulnerable. It's important.

The Apostle Paul gives us a God-prospective on this:

> Brothers, think of what you were when you were called. Not many of you were wise by human standards; not many were influential; not many were of noble birth. But God chose the foolish things of the world to shame the wise; God chose the weak things of the world to shame the strong. God chose the lowly things of this world and the despised things—and the things that are not—to nullify the things that are, so that no one may boast before him.
>
> 1 CORINTHIANS 1:26

It says God chose us, not from the pile of folks who were the wisest, or the most influential, or certainly of noble birth. He chose us from a different line altogether. He chose us from the line of foolish things and weak things—from the things that have been shamed in the world and are not so strong; from the lowly and despised things—so that when His glory is made evident in the earth, everybody will know it's His power at work in us and not our own. Hallelujah! So, if you feel disqualified, or there's a long line of people who say that you don't measure up—that you've failed too frequently or your pattern is too inconsistent—then, praise the Lord, because you are the perfect canvas for the power of God. But if you think you're from the right family, that your pedigree is flawless, your education is unchallenged, and your consistency is remarkable, then get down on your knees and say, "God, be merciful to me."

There's another doorway to deception, and its self-righteousness. Paul speaks into this:

> *Brothers, my heart's desire and prayer to God for the Israelites is that they may be saved.*

ROMANS 10:1

That's a startling statement to me. Paul is a Pharisee of the Pharisees. His love for the Jewish people is unquestioned. His tenacity in understanding the history of his people is unchallenged in his generation. Yet, in spite of their heritage and all they have delivered, and in spite of the debt owed to the Jewish people, Paul said, "My prayer for them is that they may be saved." Do you know the degree to which we rely on misplaced self-righteousness regarding our heritage—upon our heritage as a people; upon our heritage of the correctness of our theology; upon so many things? He said:

> *For I can testify about them that they are zealous for God, but their zeal is not based on knowledge. Since they did not know the righteousness that comes from God and sought to establish their own, they did not submit to God's righteousness.*

ROMANS 10:2-3

It's a startling statement. The biblical definition of self-righteousness is "attempting to establish one's own righteousness rather than relying on the righteousness that God provides." In other words, we'll do it ourselves. We'll do it through our correctness, through our morality, through our adherence to the rules. We'll begin to imagine ourselves superior—that we're more correct and we're more right. We'll fail to recognize our own vulnerability and our own inconsistency. We won't see the beam in our own eye while we're helping our neighbor find the speck in theirs. He went on to say that Christ was the end of the Law, so that there will be a righteousness for everyone who believes. He's not the end of the Law. He's the end of the law for righteousness. God didn't dumb down the Law. We are not down to three commandments. It's important to know, because we live in a time where there are many voices coming from the Church saying that a biblically informed morality is antiquated—that we shouldn't any longer imagine it to be binding upon those of us who consider ourselves to be Christ-followers. I don't think you want to stand before God and say, "I thought You were a little old fashioned." It will be an awkward conversation, and it will not go well with you.

This is not a new challenge to the human heart. Luke's Gospel presents a parable—a story, a word picture—that gives us a little window into this kind of self-righteousness where we're determined to establish it by our own merit:

> *To some who were confident of their own righteousness and looked down on everybody else, Jesus told this parable: "Two men went up to the temple to pray, one a Pharisee and the other a tax collector. The Pharisee stood up and prayed about himself: 'God, I thank you that I am not like other men-- robbers, evildoers, adulterers--or even like this tax collector. I fast twice a week and give a tenth of all I get.' But the tax collector stood at a distance. He would not even look up to heaven, but beat his breast and said, 'God, have mercy on me, a sinner.' I tell you that this man, rather than the other, went home justified before God."*

LUKE 18:9

It's a sobering statement. The tax collector was the biggest cheat in the community—an extortionist and immoral. It says that because of the attitude of his heart, he went home forgiven. But the religious person, with all of his rules and all of his regulations, and all of the minutia of his obedience, went home guilty.

If we seek to establish our own righteousness and imagine that we can earn a right standing with God through our behavior and strength of character, without being dependent upon the truth to inform our decisions—the Holy Spirit helping us examine our hearts, and the power of the redemptive work of Jesus to transform our character, which needs to be transformed in every one of us—then, we are extraordinarily vulnerable to deception.

There is another doorway to deception, and it's legalism. Legalism makes the law an end in itself. The objective is the keeping of the law—that's what keeps us. We lose sight of the real purpose for which God's Law was provided. It was a consistent challenge in Jesus' ministry. It was an objective of His to open the eyes of a generation:

> *One of them, an expert in the law, tested him with this question: "Teacher, which is the greatest commandment in the Law?" Jesus replied: "'Love the Lord your God with all your heart and with all your soul and with all your mind.' This is the first and greatest commandment. And the second is like it: 'Love your neighbor as yourself.' All the Law and the*

Prophets hang on these two commandments."

MATTHEW 22:35-40

There are more than 600 rules and regulations, and Jesus said that they all hang from those two commandments: "Love God with all your heart, with all your mind, with all your soul. And love one another—love your neighbor." Any application or interpretation of the law that doesn't produce those two forms of love is a perversion of the intent of God's Law. Clearly, people matter. Clearly, the attitude of our heart towards God matters. And anything that we raise above those two premises, we have put out of place.

To me, one of the most startling examples in Scripture is the way that Jesus' generation treated the Sabbath rules. That was a law that came from God:

> *Six days do your work, but on the seventh day do not work, so that your ox and your donkey may rest and the slave born in your household, and the alien as well, may be refreshed.*

EXODUS 23:12

Six days to work, one day to rest. Jesus consistently bumped into the challenges. In Mark's Gospel, Chapter 2 and verse 27, He said succinctly: "The Sabbath was made for man, not man for the Sabbath." They had perverted it by the time Jesus was there. They had turned it around and made it quite the opposite—that man was made for the Sabbath—and Jesus said, "You're not right." If you read the Gospels, and you don't know, you almost think that Jesus waited for the Sabbath to do miracles just to annoy the religious leaders, and it worked:

> *On a Sabbath Jesus was teaching in one of the synagogues,*
> *and a woman was there who had been crippled by a spirit for*
> *eighteen years. She was bent over and could not straighten*
> *up at all. When Jesus saw her, he called her forward and said*
> *to her, "Woman, you are set free from your infirmity." Then*
> *he put his hands on her, and immediately she straightened*
> *up and praised God. Indignant because Jesus had healed on*
> *the Sabbath, the synagogue ruler said to the people, "There*
> *are six days for work. So come and be healed on those days,*
> *not on the Sabbath."*

LUKE 13:10-14

What a happy, happy man. What a precious overseer of the community of faith. What compassion he had for the infirm. She's been attending that synagogue for years and years with no help, and he saw her delivered before his very eyes. But rather than celebrate, he was angry. A hardened heart relates very closely to spiritual blindness, for it's with the heart we perceive spiritual things. Spiritual blindness explains why so many people—even churchgoers, Christians—are nearly blind to what God is doing, because we have hard hearts, and it's left us blind. We sit and look and we don't see. Self-righteousness not only produces spiritual blindness, it also makes people blind to the reality of their own condition. It's a dangerous thing. Don't tolerate it. Don't cultivate it. Don't celebrate it. We can become so filled with pride in our spiritual correctness—in the way we move in the Spirit, in the way we worship, and in the way we read. We can take the things that are the fundamental nourishment of our lives and pervert them into points of pride that make us vulnerable. We need God's help.

The message to the church in Laodicea is a word picture of deception:

> *"You say, 'I am rich; I have acquired wealth and do not need a thing.' But you do not realize that you are wretched, pitiful, poor, blind and naked."*
>
> REVELATION 3:17

This will only increase. Before the Lord returns, deception will become an epidemic. There simply is not a pill you can take or an exercise you do once. We will have to learn to live in such a way that we love the truth. It's a necessary component for a healthy spiritual immune system. You won't remain healthy physically very long if you purposefully and intentionally compromise your immune system. There are too many things that exist on planet Earth that will destroy you, and my Bible says the thief comes to steal, to kill, and to destroy. That's his agenda, and he is good at it. He has had millennia to practice, and some of the most remarkable people of faith have been affected by him. You and I, therefore, need to do everything in our power to maintain as healthy a spiritual immune system as we know how and be dependent upon the Person of the Holy Spirit, and the truth of the Word of God, and the strength that comes to us from a community of faith. Rather than living frightened lives, I think we can live boldly for the purposes of God. In a dark and corrupt world, we can hold out the truth of the light of a Living God in a way that is a rallying point for people that are searching. Jude says to "snatch" people from the flames. We have that great privilege, but it requires an intentional purpose in our hearts to live for the glory of God and not for ourselves.

The Bible tells us that before Jesus returns there will be some "big trouble." It's referred to in Scripture as the *tribulation*. It's a very difficult season, and an attitude of a significant part of the American Church is, "I just don't have to think about that. I'll be gone before then." It's not a helpful attitude in so many, many ways. There are some primary characters that are introduced as a part of that "big trouble" in Scripture, and I want to tag them for you, because it's one of those things that will require some thought on our part. It's more than a single lesson, or the unveiling of a timeline or a chart. It will require some prayer, and some reflection, and some thought. It'll require an awareness of spiritual conditions and trends regarding what's happening in our world. It'll require a level of awareness that, candidly, has not been present in contemporary American Christendom. We just haven't been that concerned. We wanted to be certain that we've made a profession of faith and perhaps we've been baptized, but we haven't really been concerned with our Bibles, or with a God-perspective, or what holiness looks like. I don't see a great deal of evidence that wickedness and unrighteousness and immorality vex us, and I want us to reflect on the values that have captured our hearts.

Now, let's introduce the characters in this season of trouble. The most obvious is Satan, and he'll step into a more prominent role in human history than we've seen him in before. You need to know what his agenda is. It's given to us in some very clear ways in Scripture:

> *Again, the devil took him to a very high mountain and showed him all the kingdoms of the world and their splendor. "All this I will give you," he said, "if you will bow down and worship me." Jesus said to him, "Away from me, Satan! For it is written: 'Worship the Lord your God, and serve him only.'"*

MATTHEW 4:8-10

It's not uncommon that I meet people who have spent all their lives in church and question whether or not the devil exists. They're a bit too sophisticated, a bit too intellectual, and a bit too enlightened. Well, it occurs to me that if Jesus believed in Satan, perhaps you and I should, too. If the Head of the Church believes in him; if Jesus said he saw him fall from Heaven; perhaps you and I should make room in our heart, imagination, and intellect for the existence of Satan.

Listen to what Satan was trying to accomplish when he said to Jesus, "I'll give all of this to you, the kingdoms of the Earth." Jesus didn't challenge his authority over those kingdoms. Satan was trying to secure worship. He said, "If you'll worship me, I'll give that to you." Satan's goal is to be the object of worship. It was that pride that led to his initial rebellion—he wanted to be worshipped as God is worshipped. In the battle at the culmination of the ages, Satan will think he has accomplished that, having found a vehicle through which he can cause humanity to worship him. He'll be deceived in the same way in which he thought the cross was a victory. There was a celebration for that point in time when the Son of God hung on that cross, and Satan thought he had accomplished his objective.

In parallel to that, there'll be a point at the culmination of the ages when Satan will think that he has accomplished his objective and become the center of worship of all humanity. But just as the cross, in a great paradox, turned out to be a point of tremendous victory for the people of God, the point ahead at the culmination of time will become a tremendous victory for the people of God, too, because it will bring back the King.

Don't look at the season ahead of us with fear, and dread, and anxiety. Look at it with a sense of anticipation. Not every aspect of the pathway will be easy, but it is taking us toward something that is remarkable. Remember what it says about Jesus in Hebrews 12:2, "For the joy set before him, He endured the cross." He knew he was headed toward something so much better, that the pain and the agony and the suffering of the cross were inconsequential compared to what was ahead.

The Antichrist is a complex character, and it's worth every effort to learn more about that person. He will be an individual that will step on to the stage of human history—as one of the most remarkable human beings that the world will have ever seen: talented, capable, and winsome. He'll succeed in gaining an influence in our world that is unprecedented in human history. The Apostle John warns in one of his letters:

> *Dear children, this is the last hour; and as you have heard that the antichrist is coming, even now many antichrists have come. This is how we know it is the last hour.*

> 1 JOHN 2:18

Not the last day or the last season, "it is the last hour." The appearance of the Antichrist is a signal that we are nearing the culmination of the age. John continues:

> *This is how you can recognize the Spirit of God: Every spirit that acknowledges that Jesus Christ has come in the flesh is from God, but every spirit that does not acknowledge Jesus is*

not from God. This is the spirit of the antichrist, which you
have heard is coming and even now is already in the world.

1 JOHN 4:2-3

Antichrist carries with it a couple of meanings. The prefix *anti* carries with it two meanings: either "to be against" or "in place of." As I understand the scripture, both of those meanings will come into play in the individual of the Antichrist. He will stand against, but also desire to take the place of the authentic Christ. *Christ* is the English equivalent of the Greek *Christos*, which is the equivalent of the Hebrew *Mashiach* or *Messiah*—"Anointed One." The Antichrist, therefore, is the anti-Messiah or the anti-Anointed One—one who is against the Son of God.

Now, from the passages in John, we can make three deductions: 1) There is a spirit of antichrist in the world; 2) there have been many antichrists that have gone into the world; 3) there will ultimately be an individual that will be the embodiment of the spirit of antichrist at the culmination of the ages. The spirit of antichrist is at work in the earth. There is a spirit in the earth that is opposed to the Messiah and opposed to the idea of the Anointed One. And if you look across the course of human history, there are any number of individuals who seem to be an expression, or an embodiment of that spirit. Wicked, beastly, and ungodly people have stepped onto the stage of human history and wrought almost incomprehensible evil and destruction. It's uncomfortable and inconvenient to think about it. We have seen some modern expressions of that.

I think it's worth noting from the language that the spirit of antichrist doesn't emerge from paganism. It's wrong to look towards the pagan world as the primary expression of the spirit of antichrist. It clearly emerges from the context of the community of faith. Scripture says that he has gone out "from us." The ideas, language, verbiage and patterns of behavior that will ultimately be expressed in that individual will be very reminiscent of the language, behaviors, vocabularies and practices that we're familiar with in the context of church. The antichrist, the spirit of antichrist, will only arise where the claims of Jesus have been stated. It is clearly Satan's counterfeit attack.

One of the best expressions of the spirit of antichrist, or one of the earliest ones we have in Scripture, is when Pilate presents Jesus before the street in Jerusalem, and says, "It's my custom to release to you a prisoner at this time of the year, and I'll release to you Jesus of Nazareth whom they say is the Christ. Or I'll release to you Barabbas, a murderer and insurrectionist, a violent man." The people in the streets of Jerusalem had a choice that day, and through a variety of motivations, the cry arose, "Give us Barabbas." When you read the text, Pilate is incredulous. He can't believe it. He thinks he has outwitted the Jewish religious leaders, and he's put it to the street. You can tell he's confident that the man he believes to be innocent will be released, but the people scream, "Give us Barabbas." Well, I believe there's a parallel at the end of the age when God will present humanity with a choice between the true Christ and the false one, and the majority of the people in the earth, in an expression of rebellion, will say, "We choose Barabbas."

The Antichrist, the scripture tells us, will gain authority over all the earth. He'll be such a remarkable problem solver, so good at bringing people together and diminishing the barriers that have separated us, that we will willingly give him the keys of the nations. Then, for a brief season it will appear that he has solved the problems that have vexed us, until his true nature is revealed. In the book of Revelation, he's referred to as a "wild beast." That's a frightening description to me—an individual that God describes as "beastly." For a brief season of time, he will wreak havoc on humanity, and the Bible tells us that the way the Antichrist will ultimately be defeated will be at the appearance of the true Christ. There's tremendous comfort in that for me. We rest in the shadow of His protection. He watches over us.

Again, on this point, I think the American Church has had an enormous arrogance. We have liked to say that God would never allow His people to suffer. We've just pushed the discussion aside and pushed it out and ignored any passage that might lead us towards any imagination of that. That's a very difficult message to share in this day with the persecuted believers among the nations. It is presumptive to sit in the midst of our abundance, affluence, and liberties and say that God's people would never have to endure such a thing, or to imagine that we're immune. Even worse is to not recognize the grace and the mercy of God, the opportunity that's been presented to us to be advocates for Jesus.

A close associate of the Antichrist, will be a false prophet:

> *He performs great signs, so that he even makes fire come down out of heaven to the earth in the presence of men. And he deceives those who dwell on the earth because of the signs which it was given him to perform in the presence of the beast, telling those who dwell on the earth to make an image to the beast...*

REVELATION 13:13-14

He will lead the worship of the Beast, and he'll do it with religious activity and religious language and great signs and wonders. I've spent my life in the Charismatic Renewal, and there's an enormous emphasis on signs and wonders in the supernatural. I'm not opposed to those things. I'm very dependent upon them, but they are not evidence of maturity. They are not always even evidence of the presence of the Spirit of God. We need to have the wisdom and the discernment to know the difference. We've been a little casual. We've been more than a little casual. There will be a religious component to the Antichrist's reign in the earth that will capture the hearts of an overwhelming part of the population. But all of this is the precursor to the ultimate part of the story—the return of the King. In Revelation, Jesus says:

"Behold, I am coming soon! My reward is with me, and I will give to everyone according to what he has done. I am the Alpha and the Omega, the First and the Last, the Beginning and the End. Blessed are those who wash their robes, that they may have the right to the tree of life and may go through the gates into the city. Outside are the dogs, those who practice magic arts, the sexually immoral, the murderers, the idolaters and everyone who loves and practices falsehood. I, Jesus, have sent my angel to give you this testimony for the churches. I am the Root and the Offspring of David, and the bright Morning Star."

REVELATION 22:12-16

Folks, you want to be ready on that day. You want to be prepared. You want to be as prepared as young David was when he stepped into the middle of the Israelite's camp and he heard Goliath bellow his challenge. While the most valiant Israelite warriors were hiding in their tents, a teenage kid said, "Who does that man think he is?" He understood something about God, and he had worked that out—not in a public place—in a very private and lonely place while he tended a flock of sheep, doing a job that no one else wanted.

If you think you have a place in life—a station in life, an assignment in life—that is avoided by others, it can very well be a place of God's preparation in your life. Don't spend your life angry because your circumstances are imperfect. Don't be filled with resentment and bitterness because of the place where you stand. Begin to say to the Lord, "Lord, let this be Your place of preparation in my life. Open my eyes to You; unstop my ears; soften my heart; and give me a spiritual awareness, that in the midst of the difficulty, I might see You." Then, the day will come that you will hear a blatant bellowing of evil, and you'll say, "That will yield to my God," and you'll be prepared.

It's the privilege we've been given in our days under the sun. The Bible says that our life is like a breath, a vapor. It's like a flower that blooms one day and is gone the next. Let's use the strength of our days for the glory of God. Invest yourselves in the things of God. Give your heart to the things of God. Put your mind, and your resources, and your talent to work for the things of God. It's not an obligation to be fulfilled, so you can do what you want to do. It's the greatest invitation available to a human being. The privilege of being a part of the Church of Jesus Christ is the highest honor extended to us in our life under the sun. We don't want to treat it casually. It's not a frightening time, it's an exciting time. The King is coming! He's coming for a Church without spot or wrinkle, and we want to be prepared.

Pray this prayer:

Heavenly Father, I humble myself before You today to acknowledge You as the Creator of all things. You have made us. We are the sheep of Your pasture. Through Your truth we have found freedom. You have given us a home and place

of liberty. Give us the wisdom to maintain what has been entrusted to us. Let the darkness be pushed back and the light break forth in this season. Awaken Your people in this generation. You are our Hope and our great Redeemer. Let the name of Jesus be exalted and all who oppose Him stumble. In Jesus' name, amen.

GOD BLESS AMERICA AGAIN

THE PROMISES OF GOD

I. LISTENING AND UNDERSTANDING

It's important to consider these questions: What do you think God would say to you and to me today, and what would He say to the Church in the United States? What do you imagine His message would be? If you imagine yourself to be a part of the people of God, I would submit to you these are questions you should wrestle with, however awkward the implications may be. If we don't have the courage to face these questions, we're not prepared to be God's people in this season. I am of the opinion that sweeping change is ahead of us, and instead of being frightened by that, I trust the Lord that He will lead us through. That's what is really at the heart of this study, and it begins with the Word of God and the attitude we take toward Scripture.

Truthfully, I think we've treated Scripture rather casually. For a decade or more now, we've exerted a lot of energy and effort and a tremendous amount of resources to focus on the impact of climate change—on how it could impact our wellbeing on planet Earth. We've developed a curriculum at the university level to address that. We have spent billions of dollars in cultivating new energy—forms of energy that are renewable and imagined to be less harmful to the atmosphere and to our environment. I'm not suggesting that any of that is inappropriate, but I am suggesting it seems a bit odd that we have an enormous angst over the possibility of climate change, and the Church has expressed very marginal, if any interest in the efforts towards family change. God put the family system in place, and it's the fundamental building block of society. I would submit to you that the disruption of the family system, as God intended it, poses a far greater threat to the wellbeing of human beings on planet Earth than climate change ever will. That is, if we're going to live in peace, harmony, and unity, and prosper and enjoy liberty; it will be because our family systems are strong. The only way a bait and switch could take place before us is if we are unaware of the Word of God and its principles and ideas. I want to submit to you that the Bible is worthy of more than just a dutiful, casual reading from time to time. We have to begin to read the Bible and attach authority to Scripture as if it should be authoritative in our lives. We have to imagine the Bible as a source of truth.

You see, it's very popular to think the Bible is a little bit outdated, a little out of step—that there may have been a time and a place when those rather naïve values and morals were appropriate, but after all, we're a bit more sophisticated in the twenty-first century. I don't believe that to be true. So often, I think, we're frustrated by the complexity of Scripture. I would suggest another alternative. Imagine God's Word as an invitation to think and to learn about God and His character and intent for human beings on Earth. Most of us have hobbies or things we're interested in; something we invest energy in. And yet, the complexity of thought and effort required for those things, along with the resources we invest to gain some knowledge and insight into them, don't frustrate us. In fact, we're encouraged by what we're able to learn and master.

For example, if you're a baseball fan, there's a high degree of probability that you're a statistical geek. You remember batting averages and on-base percentages and all sorts of statistics—not just for contemporary players, but even for players that we can't find baseball cards of anymore. If you are interested in video games, you not only master an awareness of the software on which the games are played and what the options and the characters are, you'll develop the physical dexterity to manipulate the controls so that you can compete on a global platform with other people investing hundreds of hours in that expertise. Then, you look at people, like me, who can't make heads or tails out of it, and can't make the controls work, and you laugh at how we're an outdated leftover from another generation—maybe appropriately so. Maybe you like to fish, and you've spent a lot of energy, time, and money acquiring the tools you need. You learn the impact of weather changes and clouds, changes in barometric pressure, and the best season and life cycles of the fish that you're after, just so you can go to the lake and outsmart a carp. These things are not wicked. They're not evil, but we invest energy and effort and money and time in the things that matter to us. We're not put off by the complexity, and we intend to master them. Yet, when it comes to the Word of God, so often we act offended because we can't, with a casual 10-minute glance, interpret all of the meaning and subtly of Scripture. God would not be much of a God if He, the Creator of all the universe, would open His greatest secrets to an individual that occasionally took a glance. The Word of God is important.

A. A LIVING WORD

For the word of God is living and active. Sharper than any double-edged sword, it penetrates even to dividing soul and spirit, joints and marrow; it judges the thoughts and attitudes of the heart. Nothing in all creation is hidden from God's sight. Everything is uncovered and laid bare before the eyes of him to whom we must give account.

HEBREWS 4:12-13

Hebrews, chapter 4, contains an interesting passage. The last phrase is important. It reminds us that we will all give an account of our lives to God. The first phrase tells us that the Word of God is living and active—it's not dead, dry, and outdated. It's very much a contemporary message to this generation. I don't imagine that the unchurched would hold that idea, but I can't imagine that the Church would refuse it. The Word of God is important to us. God is watching over His Word to fulfill it.

B. FULFILLMENT IS INTENTIONAL

Look at Isaiah 55:

> *So is my word that goes out from my mouth: It will not return to me empty, but will accomplish what I desire and achieve the purpose for which I sent it.*
>
> ISAIAH 55:11

God sent His Word into the world—into the earth, into your awareness and mine—with a purpose, and He is watching over His Word to see His purpose fulfilled. It's a principle revealed to us in Scripture from Genesis to Revelation. I think some of us imagine that God shot His arrow and then went and drew a target around it and said, "See what a good shot I am?" But that's not the way the prophetic Word of God works at all. Look at Joseph's angelic encounter in Matthew, chapter 2:

> *Then after being warned by God in a dream, he left for the regions of Galilee, and came and lived in a city called Nazareth. This was to fulfill what was spoken through the*

prophets: "He shall be called a Nazarene."

MATTHEW 2:22-23

It's a reference to Jesus made hundreds of years before His birth, and in a dream God warns Joseph, who has the responsibility of caring for the young infant. He's already been hunted. Hundreds of babies in Bethlehem have been murdered by Herod who was trying to destroy Jesus, and Joseph is appropriately wary while trying to decide where to rear his family. It says Joseph is warned by God—given instructions by God in a dream to go to the village of Nazareth, because the prophets had said the Messiah would be called a Nazarene. Not a Nazarite—a Nazarite is a Jewish sect based on compliance to a certain set of rules. You could be a Nazarite and live in any part of Israel. You could be a Nazarite and be an American, or a Brit, or a South African. To be a Nazarene you have to come from the village of Nazareth. Now why is that significant? Well, first century Nazareth had a population of less than fifteen hundred people. It was a tiny little place. And hundreds of years before the birth of the Messiah, the prophets had said the Messiah will come from Nazareth. God was watching over the most subtle details of His Word to see it fulfilled, and He still is. He's watching over His Word in your life and mine just as certainly as He watched over it in the life of Jesus. There's something of tremendous comfort and authority in that. It's good to know that God keeps His promises.

C. GOD KEEPS HIS PROMISES

The author of Hebrews, chapter 6, says,

> *When God made his promise to Abraham, since there was no*
> *one greater for him to swear by, he swore by himself, saying,*
> *"I will surely bless you and give you many descendants."*
> *And so after waiting patiently, Abraham received what*
> *was promised.*

HEBREWS 6:13-15

I don't know why God asks us to wait patiently. You know, sometimes God has asked me to wait, and I waited, but I didn't do it patiently. Have you ever done that? I waited complainingly. I waited grumpily. I waited with my fist clenched and my feet tapping and with a lot of anger building in me. That's not a very fruitful way to wait, but it says that Abraham waited patiently and God fulfilled His promise in his life. He told Abraham that all the nations of the earth, all the peoples of the earth, would be blessed through him. That's an amazing promise. It's almost unimaginable. It isn't just rhetorical. It isn't just poetic language. In Hebrews 11, it says this when speaking of Abraham:

> *By faith he made his home in the promised land like a stranger*
> *in a foreign country; he lived in tents, as did Isaac and Jacob,*
> *who were heirs with him of the same promise.*

HEBREWS 11:9

Now, the promise God made to Abraham is in the book of Genesis. This is Hebrews 11. It's the Hall of Fame of Faith of men and women in the Bible; and it says that Abraham is a man of faith, and God kept His promise. But it says something more—that Isaac and Jacob were heirs of the same promise. Isaac, Abraham's son, and Jacob, his grandson, were heirs to the same promise that had been made to Abraham. Now, why do we care? Why does that matter to us? Well, look at Galatians 3:

If you belong to Christ, then you are Abraham's seed, and heirs according to the promise.

GALATIANS 3:29

You see, if we are in Christ—if we are Christ-followers—the promise God made to Abraham in the early chapters in the book of Genesis is relevant to you and me all these years later. It means that just as much as God honored His promise in the life of Isaac or Jacob, He will honor it in your life or in my life. Our attitude towards God makes a difference. God is watching over His promises. In Galatians 3, it further says,

He redeemed us in order that the blessing given to Abraham might come to the Gentiles through Christ Jesus, so that by faith we might receive the promise of the Spirit.

GALATIANS 3:14

Most of us as Christians would put a period there and we would talk a great deal about the redemptive power of God—Jesus' substitutionary death on a cross, His resurrection to life again—that we might be justified. He redeemed us. Period. But that's not how the sentence is written, is it? It says, "He redeemed us in order that the blessing given to Abraham might come to the Gentiles [the non-Jews] through Christ Jesus, so that by faith we might receive the promise of the Spirit." The redemptive purpose of Jesus included the blessing of Abraham being extended to all people. God is concerned with His promises and seeing them extended to anyone who will believe them.

Look at God's promise in 2 Peter 3:

But in keeping with his promise we are looking forward to a new heaven and a new earth, the home of righteousness.

2 PETER 3:13

Did you know there's a new Heaven and a new Earth coming? It's a promise of God. It will be a place where righteousness—a right standing with God—prevails. Isaiah, the prophet, says it more poetically. He says that the lion will lay down with the lamb, and the child will play at the den of the cobra (Isaiah 11:6-8), and we'll beat our swords into plow shares (Isaiah 2:4), because we'll make war no more. Sounds pretty good, doesn't it? It's a promise. God is faithful. He will keep His promises. A more germane question is how well do you know them? Because if you don't know them, it's highly improbable that you'll trust Him to fulfill them in your life. Then, you're just living randomly, accidentally. It's not a good way to live.

II. ISRAEL, ISLAM, AND THE MIDDLE EAST

Now, I want to unpack a promise that is central to the story of Scripture, and it deals with current events in some rather profound ways. I want to look at Israel, Islam, and the Middle East—how they impact God's perspective on our world in this generation, and what some of those implications are for you and for me.

A. JEWISH PEOPLE & THE LAND OF ISRAEL

1. PROMISED

We're going to start with the Jewish people in the land of Israel:

The Lord said to Abram after Lot had parted from him, "Lift up your eyes from where you are and look north and south, east and west. All the land that you see I will give to you and your offspring forever."

GENESIS 13:14-15

You ought to circle that last word. God said to Abram: "I will give this land—a place on planet Earth, a specific plot of ground—to you and your offspring forever." Again, it would help the U.N. if somebody would send them that verse. There is tremendous consternation in the earth about the Jewish people occupying a little piece of land at the end of the Mediterranean, and God said as early as the very beginning chapters of the Bible: "That land belongs to the descendants of Abraham, Isaac and Jacob forever." And God, quite candidly, doesn't care what opposing voices declare or what I think. He made that promise, and He'll keep it.

But I believe there is a far more profound lesson in that for you and for me: The right of the Jewish people to live in that Promised Land—the inheritance that God gave to them—is not without condition. In fact, it is a very conditional promise. God said their right to live in that land is dependent upon their relationship with Him. It's important for you and for me to understand that many, if not most, of the promises of God to you and to me are conditional promises. We have to meet the condition to receive the benefit of the promise. I'll give you an example from the book of Romans:

If you confess with your mouth and believe in your heart that Jesus is Lord, you'll be saved.

ROMANS 10:9

Will everybody be saved? No. Why not? It's a conditional promise. It says, "If you believe in your heart and confess with your mouth." You see, what God provided for us through Jesus' death, burial, and resurrection, while it is universally available, it doesn't mean it will be universally received. There's a condition for the promise.

I'll give you another one in 1 John:

> *If we confess our sins, God is faithful and just to forgive us and to cleanse us from all unrighteousness.*

1 JOHN 1:9

God has made provision so that your sins and my sins—the darkest part of our ungodliness—do not have the power to separate us from the Kingdom of God. But we have to meet the condition, don't we? If we don't confess our sin, if we don't acknowledge our need for a savior, if we don't come in humble repentance, we don't receive the benefit of the promise.

Well, in a similar way, the Jewish people were promised a piece of land, and God said they would flourish in that land as long as they honored Him. And He made supernatural provision for them. You know the story. He took them from Egyptian slavery, and brought them through the wilderness. While in a desert with no natural resources for provision, God provided everything they needed, from manna for them to eat, to the pillar of cloud and the pillar of fire to direct and protect them. When necessary, God brought water from a rock in the midst of a brutally parched desert. And when He moved them into the Promised Land, He said, "I'll sustain you in this land in the same way I sustained you in the desert. I'll bring rain to the land when you need. You will prosper here. You will flourish here in a way no people on the planet will ever flourish here other than you." Then, Joshua led them into the Promised Land, and they occupied it.

For hundreds of years, they lived in the land of Israel with no central government, with no monarchy—God was their King. It's the period of the Judges, and there's a book in your Bible with that name. The Judges were leaders, whom God raised up from time to time—heroic people, people of remarkable gifts and abilities—they're almost like comic book characters. Gideon was a judge. With three hundred men he overcame an army of thousands of adversaries. Samson was a judge—a crazy strong guy. But there's a pattern in the book of Judges. God would bless the Israelites, and they would flourish. And in their prosperity and their abundance, their hearts would drift away from God. They would begin to act like all the other people groups around them, and they would forfeit their blessings. Their enemies would begin to overtake them, and they would cry out to God for mercy, and God would raise up a judge—a Samson or a Gideon or a Debra—and there would be deliverance. Subsequently, there would be a time of fruitfulness and prosperity, and then they would begin to drift again. The book of Judges comprises a period of almost four hundred years where that pattern is repeated over, and over, and over again—more than twice as long as the United States has been a nation—and God didn't drive them from the land. They would suffer in seasons, but God would restore them and realign things, and they would understand. Then, they would drift again.

The last of the Judges is Samuel. There are two books in the Bible that bear his name. You know him as a prophet, but he's the last of the judges. The tribal leaders came to Samuel and said, "We don't like this arrangement we've had with God as our King. We want to be like all the other nations." And Samuel said, "Okay," and God appointed a king. They rejected God, and in His grace and His mercy He said, "I'll recruit a king for you." He chose Saul, and when Saul in his pride turned his back on God, God chose a second King, David—a remarkable man— the greatest of all the Israelite Kings. David was a man with a heart so uniquely turned toward the Lord that God said to him: "Your descendants will sit on the throne of Israel forever." The Messiah came from the line of David. God chose that king for them. Yet for hundreds of years, with the monarchy in place in Israel, the children of Israel continued to drift further, and further, and further away from God. They even lost the Book of the Law. They were doing a remodel on the Temple, and they found it buried in the wall. It had been hidden, and nobody missed it. That was during King Josiah's reign. When they found the Book in the wall next to the Temple on the Temple Mount, there were also shrines for prostitution—male and female—to the fertility gods of the Canaanites. They had drifted a *long* way.

So, for hundreds of years, God responded to them in short seasons, but finally God said to them, "It's enough. You can't stay here anymore. We're done and you're leaving." And in 721 B.C., the Assyrian armies destroyed the northern kingdom of Israel. Some 150 years later, the southern kingdom didn't learn their lesson and the Babylonians came. Nebuchadnezzar brought his armies, and they destroyed the city of Jerusalem and the Temple. In fact, you read in the books of the prophets, Jeremiah and Ezekiel, messages that deal with that. Jeremiah is the one sounding the warning that destruction and captivity are coming: "You're going to leave. You're not going to stay anymore." Ezekiel is the prophet that spoke to the Israelites while they were in exile. For seventy years, they didn't live in the land anymore. God said, "It's your land, but you can't stay there." And then He brought them back. Nehemiah comes back to Jerusalem and rebuilds the wall. Then, in the book that bears his name, Ezra, the priest, came back and reinstituted priestly worship in the Temple in Jerusalem. And they began to flourish again until we open the New Testament.

Some people say that in the New Testament God took a chill pill—that He's a little more laid back. They haven't read it very carefully. When Jesus is coming down the Mount of Olives, the city of Jerusalem is spread before Him, and He begins to weep.

His heart is broken. He said, "If you had only recognized the time of God's coming to you. But you didn't recognize it. And now, their armies are going to encircle you." In the first century, the most effective means of warfare was siege warfare. The armies would literally encircle a city—no food in, no food out; no one in, no one out. And Jesus said, "The armies will encircle you, and they will take your babies and dash their heads against the rocks. You can't stay here anymore," He said, "Your hearts are so far from Me."

Within a generation of Jesus' death and resurrection, in 70 C.E., the Roman Legion encircled the city of Jerusalem and did precisely what Jesus had forewarned. They razed the Temple, destroyed the city, and slaughtered many of the inhabitants. Then 60 years later, the Romans made it illegal for a Jew to even live in Jerusalem. They'd had enough of their rebellions. For 2,000 years, the Jewish people were spread to the four corners of the planet. They had no nation. They had no national homeland. There was nothing to bind them together except their heritage, and inexplicably, apart from God, they survived.

2. RESTORED

"This is what the LORD says—your Redeemer, who formed you in the womb: I am the LORD, who has made all things, who alone stretched out the heavens, who spread out the

earth by myself...who carries out the words of his servants
and fulfills the predictions of his messengers, who says of
Jerusalem, 'It shall be inhabited,' of the towns of Judah, 'They
shall be built,' and of their ruins, 'I will restore them...'"

ISAIAH 44:24, 26

It was 1948, the end of World War II, when the horrors of the Holocaust started to become more broadly recognized across the world—and there was a bit of sentiment for the Jewish people to have someplace to go. Their homes had been confiscated. Their wealth had been confiscated. Six million of them had died in the Holocaust, and there was enough international compassion that there was a movement for the nation of Israel to be reinstated. It was May of 1948—after the U.N. had made that decision through tremendous effort and support from the United States, and particularly from President Harry Truman—that the modern state of Israel was acknowledged. Immediately, the surrounding Arab nations declared war on them—nations that had standing armies with centralized governments and economies. Israel had none of those things, and supernaturally, miraculously, Israel survived. Now, over 70 years later, tiny Israel continues to flourish. There are about six million Jews in the land of Israel today. They've come from all the nations of the world. There are another million Israeli citizens that are Arabs, and they have flourished in the midst of an environment that today is seething in violence and hatred.

"Hear the word of the LORD, O nations; proclaim it in distant coastlands: 'He who scattered Israel will gather them and will watch over his flock like a shepherd.'"

JEREMIAH 31:10

3. WILL FLOURISH

The Prophet Isaiah looks toward a day when Israel will once again thrive:

"In that day: 'Sing about a fruitful vineyard: I, the LORD, watch over it [Israel]*; I water it continually. I guard it day and night so that no one may harm it; ...In days to come Jacob will take root, Israel will bud and blossom and fill all the world with fruit.'"*

ISAIAH 27:2-3, 6

You might say, "Well, it's very poetic language. Isaiah, after all, writes with a flourish." But that's more than poetry, because today Israel provides some of the finest fruits and vegetables and herbs for the markets of Europe. They are the most valuable fruits and vegetables. There's an irony in that, because for hundreds of years when the Jewish people lived in Europe, in many instances, they weren't allowed to own property. They couldn't farm. They couldn't have a garden. It's the reason they were merchants and shopkeepers. Anti-Semitism is an ancient hatred. It's not a new thing.

Anti-Semitism is the hatred of the Jewish people. Shakespeare, for all of his brilliance, was anti-Semitic. His character, Shylock was greedy, money grubbing, and oh, coincidentally, a Jewish person.

When they began to immigrate back to the land of Israel at the beginning of the twentieth century, they had to learn to farm again. It shouldn't be lost on a casual observer that Israel, today, leads the world in agricultural technology and implementation. They have literally caused the desert to bloom. So, when Isaiah said that they will "fill the world with their fruit," it wasn't just a poetic turn of a phrase. It was a God- perspective that you and I have watched come into existence in our lifetime. It's a remarkable story.

B. IMPLICATIONS FOR USA

1. A PROMISE AND A WARNING

Now, I think there's a lesson for us with the land of Israel, because the Jewish people didn't have the privilege of living in the land if they chose to ignore the principles of God. Remember, America is not a nation defined by ethnicity. America is a melting pot of immigrants, and immigration has always been our strength. We are a nation that is defined by an idea, a principle, because we have come from all the nations of the world—not a particular ethnicity or ideology—but there's been an "idea" that caused America to be great, and it is grounded and rooted in the principles of God. Our legal system, our educational system, and our cultural values have all been derived from Scripture, and we have prospered uniquely. Our people have come here from all the nations in the world, and typically we've come because we weren't succeeding where we were. We've come here destitute, with hope in our hearts, and God has poured out His blessings upon us. So, if God has blessed America, and I believe He has, do we imagine that we will continue to enjoy liberty and freedom and abundance and blessings if we continue to turn our backs on God?

I don't expect people outside the Church to embrace that idea, but folks, inside the Church we have an assignment. We're the conscience of the culture. We are the voice for Truth. We have to be willing to be distinctive, not because of our bizarre behavior, but because of the values that we hold. Israel is a powerful reminder of that. God can enable us to flourish in the midst of tremendous adversity and hatred if we will choose Him, but if we turn our backs on Him, we will forfeit our liberty.

2. A TOUGH NEIGHBORHOOD

I want to take a minute with the Middle East. I think it's helpful. We'll start with Israel. It's a tiny little nation at the end of the Mediterranean. It really is a small place. It's not much bigger than Middle Tennessee. You can make a drive around Israel in a half a day and not hurry. As I said, about six million Jews live there, and another million Israelis are Arabs. So, a small population is surrounded by an enormous mass of Muslim nations—tens of millions of inhabitants occupying those nations—and this entire mass is determined, committed and dedicated to the annihilation and the destruction of the State of Israel. It's not just a political issue. Islam is far more than just a religion. Islam is territorial. Islam is a worldview, an ideology. It's linked to the possession of land as a religious expression. In other words, if a piece of property ever comes under Islamic control, the Koran teaches that it belongs to the Islamic world forever. If they fail to inhabit it in a season, whoever is occupying that land is an intruder, and they are commanded to drive them out of that land. Now, it's worth noting that King David was king in Jerusalem more than 1,500 years before Mohammed was born. It is true that the Muslims occupied the land of Israel for a season, so when the United Nations chose to give a little sliver of land to the Jewish people that had at one time been under Muslim control, it was an offense to the Islamic nations, and could not be tolerated. Therefore, we've been told for the decades since Israel's existence, that the removal of the State of Israel would bring peace to the Middle East. Because after all, we are told that Islam is peaceful.

I want to unpack that with you. I don't doubt that there are places in the world where Islam is peaceful—predominantly where Islam exists in nations that have an infrastructure that provides peace, and Islam lives beneath that. In the places where Islam is the predominant influence, they don't seem to be so peaceful. Egypt was one of the most stable nations of the Middle East for many, many years. It was the most populated because the Nile River provided a stable water source, which is the most precious resource in the Middle East, not petroleum. Egypt was the most western of all the Middle Eastern nations for many, many years. Egyptian President Mubarak was a great friend of the West. Now, he wasn't a great man—he was oppressive, authoritarian and could be brutal, but he caused Egypt to be a western leaning nation in the Middle East. He established and maintained a peace with Israel.

Then, things changed in 2011. Remember the Arab Spring? It started at the end of 2010, but it was 2011 when the Arab Spring came to Egypt. We saw Tahrir Square filled with predominantly young people. Our media was full of social media posts coming from Egypt. We said it was an Arab Spring; it was a new beginning. Peace and tolerance and cooperation had come to the Middle East, and we turned our back on Mubarak. In less than two weeks he was gone—ousted. Then, it wasn't too long, within 18 months, that the Muslim Brotherhood seized control of Egypt, and they began a rather systematic oppression of those who didn't agree with them—the Christians, but it was not limited to Christians. The Egyptian military is the most powerful force in Egypt. They controlled the economy then and today, and they managed to oust the Muslim Brotherhood and take back control of their nation. They brought some stability back to Egypt, but they did it over the objections of our US government.

Adjacent to Egypt is Libya. Libya, if you don't know, is where Benghazi is. You've heard a bit about Benghazi; Americans were killed there. Libya was ruled during that season by Muammar Kaddafi, another bad guy. He was a brutal authoritarian ruler. For a season, he sponsored terrorism throughout Europe until President Reagan sent some bombers in his direction, and after that he kind of stayed home. The United States lead a coalition against Kaddafi and ousted him in Libya, after which the country deteriorated, with no central government, into a chaotic incubator for terrorism that quickly spread all over the region.

Now, those aren't the only examples. We can move to the nations you probably know a bit better, like Iraq. We have invested an enormous amount of life and treasure into Iraq, and our finest young men and women are there. It's not a peaceful place today. It has been the incubator for ISIS. Al Qaeda was replaced by ISIS, and ISIS will be replaced by something else. At one time there were 100,000 Iranian-supported troops in Iraq. It's a very unstable place.

Then, there is Iran, a large nation that was formerly known as ancient Persia, where Queen Esther lived. The hatred between the Persian people and the Jewish people is not a new thing; it's not a twenty-first century invention. Iran is agreed to be, by the international community, the primary state sponsor of terrorism on planet Earth. They fund groups like Hezbollah and provide the military resources and the infrastructure needed for those terrorist groups to flourish in this region and around the world. The United States has previously, and in this century, treated Iran as if they're our best friend in this entire region. We created a clear path for the Iranians to have nuclear weapons, and we provided them with hundreds of billions of dollars to help fund that initiative, while turning our backs to a great degree on Israel and the Jewish people. Simultaneously, our government worked actively to unseat the Israeli Prime Minister in an election.

A neighbor to Iraq is Syria, and they have for years been embroiled in a civil war. Hundreds of thousands of civilians were destroyed in Syria. West of Syria is Lebanon, a tiny and beautiful nation. At one time, it was a Christian Arab nation in the Middle East. Lebanon has no central government. Hezbollah, a terrorist organization, is the most powerful force in the nation of Lebanon today.

If you look at this region on a map—Iraq, Syria, and Lebanon— although there are still lines on the map that identify them as nations, those nations don't exist any longer. The map hasn't been redrawn yet. There isn't a consensus internationally or globally.

The battle is still going on regarding who's really going to reside over this region or territory, but the lines that have been drawn on that map, and that have been in place since World War I, are erased. That part of the world is up for grabs. That's what you have seen being played out in the news for many years, but the part that gets less airplay has to do with the Christian communities in Iraq and Syria and in this part of the world.

Iraq's Nineveh Plains are home to some of the oldest Christian communities in all the world, and they have been systematically hunted down, driven out, and given no recourse. Now, the refugees that we at one time saw streaming into Europe—hundreds of thousands of them—were typically young, Muslim refugees. The Christians in these places have had their churches destroyed, along with all the archaeological centers. These powers have done everything they could do to annihilate and eliminate any semblance of the existence of Christianity. And yet, the United Nations did not welcome the Christian refugees. If they can be identified as victims of a genocide and they can be lumped in with the Yazidis and some other people groups, perhaps they'll be tolerated as refugees, but they will not be given refugee status just as Christians. And the world looks on with a kind of an addled confusion, "What do we do?" It's more than a bit ironic.

Now, let's look at the West Bank. It is so called because it's on the western bank of the Jordan River. The West Bank had been under Jordanian control prior to the Six Day War in 1967 when it came under Israeli control. For decades since then, it has become the sore spot for peace in the Middle East. There have been all sorts of summits at the White House, in Oslo, Norway, and in various places in the planet based on the thinking that the Palestinian refugees were the reason there was unrest in the Middle East: "If that group of people could just be settled, we could have peace in the Middle East." It was the attitude expressed by the Muslim world, and in recent years, we have seen hundreds of thousands of Muslim refugees being driven into Europe and every place in the world. They want us to take them into the United States.

Now, they're not making room for them in any part of the Middle East. In spite of the petroleum wealth and all the resources and the alignment of ideology and worldview, they insist that they be welcomed into Europe and into the United States and other places in the world, while there has been no willingness, no heartburn to resolve the Palestinian problem, the big problem in the Middle East. It's absurd. It's illogical. In fact, it's so illogical I don't believe there is an explanation for it other than from a spiritual perspective. I've told you on many occasions that the most powerful forces in the world are spiritual. I'm not denying or diminishing political force, or economic might, or all the other expressions of power in the world. I'm simply suggesting to you that they pale in comparison to spiritual power.

3. RESPONSIBILITY

The LORD had said to Abram, "Leave your country, your
people and your father's household and go to the land I will
show you.

I will make you into a great nation,
and I will bless you;
I will make your name great,
and you will be a blessing.
I will bless those who bless you,
and whoever curses you I will curse;
and all peoples on earth
will be blessed through you."

GENESIS 12:1-3

The Church of Jesus Christ has a role to play in the earth.
Ultimately, peace in the Middle East will only come with the
Prince of Peace, but there are some implications for our nation
and how we respond to the nation of Israel and the Jewish
people based on the promises of God. We are given instructions
in the Scripture to pray for the peace of Jerusalem. It doesn't
mean that the inhabitants of Jerusalem are always perfect or
always innocent any more than the Church is always perfect
or always innocent. But God has made promises, and He's
watching over them. One of the most powerful things you and
I can choose to do is align ourselves with the purposes and the

promises of God.

We have an assignment in this nation, folks. You have no imagination how important you are. It's not just about where you sit on Sunday morning for a few minutes, or a dress code you embrace, or a beverage list you prefer. Your choice to honor God, to cooperate with His perspective, to cooperate with a God-view and align yourself with it, can bring the blessings of God to a whole nation. You are salt and light. You bring meaning and flavor to the world. And it doesn't really matter how intense the darkness is, if we will turn up the light.

When God made His promise to Abraham He said, "Look up at the sky and look at the stars in the night" (Genesis 15:5). Have you looked at a night sky lately? It's dotted with stars, and most of them are hundreds of millions of miles away. I mean, almost an unimaginable distance, and yet the light penetrates that enormous distance and that vast gulf of darkness, so that you and I can see it. I don't think it was just a random metaphor that God used with Abraham. We may live in a season when there is intense darkness, but the light you represent can penetrate that darkness over incredible distances. You matter. Your life matters. Your God-choices matter. You are not insignificant or unimportant. Tiny little Israel, with their tiny little population, captures the attention of the world because they are an expression of the purposes of God. So, too, is the Church of Jesus Christ.

Pray this prayer:

Heavenly Father, be merciful to our nation. You have uniquely blessed us. We have enjoyed freedom, abundance, protection, and great liberty. Yet, we have turned our backs on You. In our pride and arrogance, we have imagined our wealth and power have made us strong. Forgive us for our arrogance and rebellion. Do not look upon us in anger. Pour out Your Spirit upon our nation once again. Only You, Almighty God, can deliver us and make us clean. We turn to You, our God and our Redeemer. Amen.

LIFT THE NAME OF JESUS HIGH

There's a little chorus that many of us know, "Lift the Name of Jesus High," and I walk around so many days with that streaming in my head. I have this figurative image in my head, which I would love to see quite literally materialize—the name of Jesus lifted up high over our community. Now, in recent years, we have affixed "Jesus Is Lord" magnets on our cars, flown a little single engine plane over the area at Easter with a "He Is Risen" banner, and even launched hot air balloons, but I would love to see "Jesus Is Lord" floating literally above our city. I don't have a better solution for the ills that face us and the challenges that are before us, than lifting high the name of Jesus. It's at the name of Jesus, in the end, that every knee will bow and every tongue confess that Jesus Christ is Lord (Romans 14:11). It's the only resolution, ultimately. The book of Revelation tells us that things will become so intense, so horrific, and so beastly, that the only way that the destruction of humanity can be withheld is with the return of the Prince of Peace. The return of Jesus isn't a frightening thing or a fearful thing. He will come because there is no other resolution, and we will be desperate for His return. Being prepared for that season isn't about being frightened or scolded. I have wrestled with this, because I don't want this topic to be scolding. That's not helpful. I am hopeful. In fact, I am greatly anticipating what is ahead of us, not terrified by it. I believe that we are living in a season where there are unique opportunities to make an impact for the Kingdom God, and I'm grateful that God didn't choose you and me to live in just a time of "maintenance." It's a season of some significant movements of the Spirit of God. What a privilege!

I want to start in Revelation 12. If I had to look for one passage that summarizes much of what I expect in this season that we're in, I'd probably choose this passage:

> *And there was war in heaven. Michael and his angels fought against the dragon, and the dragon and his angels fought back. But he was not strong enough, and they lost their place in heaven. The great dragon was hurled down—that ancient serpent called the devil, or Satan, who leads the whole world astray. He was hurled to the earth, and his angels with him. Then I heard a loud voice in heaven say: "Now have come the salvation and the power and the kingdom of our God, and the authority of his Christ. For the accuser of our brothers, who accuses them before our God day and night, has been hurled down. They overcame him by the blood of the Lamb*

*and by the word of their testimony; they did not love their
lives so much as to shrink from death. Therefore rejoice, you
heavens and you who dwell in them! But woe to the earth
and the sea, because the devil has gone down to you! He is
filled with fury, because he knows that his time is short."*

REVELATION 12:7-12

I think that's a pretty accurate description of our world these
days. I think Satan is alive and well on planet Earth with all
of his host. That's not weird to me. It's a fundamental biblical
principle. If you're too sophisticated to believe in the devil, go
back and read what Jesus had to say. He believed in the devil.
Maybe we should. It says that there's a war in Heaven and that
Satan lost his place there. In verse 10, there's a timing phrase
that is worth noting. It's says, "Now have come the salvation
and the power and the kingdom of our God, and the authority
of his Christ." Now has come the authority of the Messiah,
the incarnate son of God. That phrase captures my attention:
"Now in the earth have come some things: salvation, power, the
Kingdom of our God, and the authority of the Son of God."
They are present in the earth. Now, the Kingdom isn't fully come;
Jesus gave us a prayer with regard to that, but we see it emerging.
The day is coming when that Kingdom will be established and
His will will be done on earth to the same extent it's done in
Heaven. Isn't that what He taught us to pray? Isn't that good to
know? When you see things changing, don't wring your hands

in fear. Get excited! It doesn't mean it's necessarily an easy path, but something good is ahead of us.

The notion of authority is worth unpacking for just a moment. In Luke 4, it's a part of Jesus' temptation. He's in the wilderness fasting—you remember the story—and Satan comes to tempt Him:

> *The devil led him up to a high place and showed him in an instant all the kingdoms of the world. And he said to him, "I will give you all their authority and splendor, for it has been given to me, and I can give it to anyone I want to."*
>
> LUKE 4:5-6

Jesus didn't challenge him. Satan said, "I have the authority over the kingdoms of this world." The psalmist says that the kings of the earth gather together and plot against God and He looks from Heaven (Psalm 2:2). Do you remember how God responds? It says that He laughs. He doesn't chuckle. He doesn't chortle. It's like a belly laugh at the naive plans of incompetent children. God looks at their efforts and He laughs, nevertheless, they do have an authority in the earth.

In Luke 10, Jesus is coaching His disciples and training them towards their ultimate assignment:

> *The seventy-two returned with joy and said, "Lord, even the*

demons submit to us in your name." He replied, "I saw Satan
fall like lightning from heaven. I have given you authority
to trample on snakes and scorpions and to overcome all the
power of the enemy; nothing will harm you."

LUKE 10:17-19

Verse 18 sounds a lot like the passage in Revelation 12, doesn't it? A significant portion of Jesus' ministry was helping those who put their faith in Him open their hearts and minds to the authority that was available to them. We've played church too long. We've convened religious gatherings and held polite little Bible studies, and we have worked on the subtleties of our theological constructs and frameworks. But we've had no imagination that there was really any authority in what we have done. We have acted as if the authority was in all the other realms of our lives. I'm not arguing it's the only authority. I'm simply arguing that it is the ultimate authority. It's unfortunate if we, the Church, who are entrusted with the ultimate authority of an Almighty God, are more cognizant of the other expressions of authority that are available to the secular culture, than we are to the authority that has been invested in us.

In Matthew 28, Jesus appears to His disciples post-resurrection:

Then Jesus came to them and said, "All authority in heaven
and on earth has been given to me. Therefore go and make
disciples of all nations, baptizing them in the name of the

Father and of the Son and of the Holy Spirit, and teaching
them to obey everything I have commanded you. And surely I
am with you always, to the very end of the age."

MATTHEW 28:18-20

There is a purpose for the authority God has invested in you and me. Did you hear it? Jesus says, "All authority in heaven and on earth has been given to me. Therefore go and make disciples of all nations." He understands there are barriers and obstacles to that and hurdles to be negotiated. He understands there's an adversary in the earth that opposes the purposes of God. Jesus, from the season of His birth until His resurrection, is confronted with the adversary opposing the purposes of God in His life on the earth. And yet He says to His followers: "All authority has been given to me now." In Revelation 1:18, He says, "I hold the keys of death and Hades." The purpose of the authority invested in us is to make disciples: "So now, you go. I'm giving you an assignment."

Now, go back and look at what Revelation 12, verse 11, says about the believers on the earth: "They overcame him [Satan] by the blood of the Lamb and by the word of their testimony." If our purpose is to make disciples, what is the process? It's important. If you only know the objective, and you don't know how you're going to get there, you're ill-equipped; you're not fully prepared. In that eleventh verse, Jesus gave us a window into the process. He said that the believers on earth would "overcome"

Satan—that he's in the earth—and we'll overcome Satan "by the blood of the Lamb and by the word of our testimony." The process, I believe, is in that word, *overcoming*. You see, I don't like that. I wish Jesus would have said, "We will have dessert and the enemy will flee before us." As I scream for more hot chocolate sauce, the enemy will tremble. But He said that we'll have to overcome him. That presupposes opposition, obstacles, and resistance, which all have to be overcome.

The book of Revelation—the story of the culmination of the age and the inheritance coming to the believers in the earth—begins and concludes with the theme of "being overcomers." I have no message of hope for you that doesn't include the willingness to overcome. Now, that isn't frightening; in overcoming we gain strength. In fact, it's impossible to gain physical strength unless you exercise, typically to the point of fatigue. If you don't exercise enough to get tired, you won't gain new strength; you'll just get a little weary. But if you'll exercise to the point of fatigue, there are all sorts of benefits. You gain greater muscle strength and greater cardio-vascular endurance. It brings about a transformation. If you don't have a mind-set and experience in the context of your spiritual life, regarding pursuing and holding your faith— standing and persevering to the point of fatigue—you're not going to gain strength. I think we have packaged Christianity as more of an entertainment module, rather than something that's intended to strengthen the Body of Christ.

Now, that may have been our past, but we're changing. We

intend to gain strength. There are people praying three to six hours a day around our church during various seasons. That takes diligence and perseverance. There are other things that could be done with their time, but they're giving their time and energy to that pursuit because they think it's valuable. There are others spending dozens of hours every week investing in preparations to teach children a meaningful faith. They are not satisfied just to convene a baby-sitting culture on Saturday night, Sunday morning, Wednesday and Thursday, or whenever they're here. They're focusing their minds, creativity, and efforts into establishing an environment that will help our children be shaped by faith and values, and form a character that will enable them to be overcomers. Those are valuable things. They are not insignificant. In your life, whatever challenges you face, you have a decision whether to retreat, coalesce, submit, yield, or decide to be an overcomer, and Scripture tells us that the objective is to overcome our adversary.

Now, we have two tools: the blood of the Lamb and the word of our testimony. I learned an explanation of that when I was a boy, and I've never been able to improve upon it. It uses the imagery of the Passover in Egypt, which was the last night for the Hebrews in Egypt after 400 years there. They've seen the devastation of the plagues, and Pharaoh's heart is still hardened. Finally, Moses says to the people: "Every family, get a lamb and then roast it. And when you slaughter the lamb, capture the blood in a basin and take hyssop (a common weed in the region) and take the blood and put it on the doorpost of your house." Moses told them that they were to eat this meal prepared in haste, warning them: "Death is coming through Egypt, and in every household where no blood is on the doorpost, the firstborn will die." Do you imagine that there were any Israelites who failed to cooperate with Moses' instruction? Absolutely— what are the chances of one-hundred percent participation in any broad group of people? Slim to none. So, it wasn't just the Egyptians that faced death. When the sun came up in the morning, there was horror in the land. Every Egyptian household was touched by death. Can you imagine the fear that would grip the people? It's the imagery that I see in Revelation 12. We take the blood of the Lamb, and we don't put it on the doorpost of our homes any longer, we apply it to the doorposts of our lives with the word of our testimony.

In the beginning chapters of Genesis, there is a delivery system for the authority and the power of God in creation—it's His Word. Repetition is a way of enforcing an idea, and over and over it says, "God said," and then there was an outcome. When you put God's Word in your mouth, it's not some mystical thing that you conjure up. God is not a heavenly vending machine that dispenses what you want. What nonsense to think that you could manipulate God with His Word! But if you will allow the Word of God to begin to shape your heart, then what comes out of your heart expresses God's power. Jesus taught us something about our words, didn't He? He said, "The words that come out of our mouth are simply the overflow from what's in our heart." If you'll put God's perspective in your heart, it will begin to shape the words that come out of you, and that is the expression of the power of God over your life. If you'll listen to what you're saying, you'll find out what you value.

In Revelation 12, verse 11, we're given the process for becoming overcomers. Then, finally, in verse 12 it says:

> *"Therefore rejoice, you heavens and you who dwell in them! But woe to the earth and the sea, because the devil has gone down to you! He is filled with fury, because he knows that his time is short."*

REVELATION 12:12

I have come to understand something as I have worked on this study; there are brief expressions that carry great meaning. When God said, through the prophet Isaiah, that the fruit of Israel would feed the nations, that wasn't a throwaway phrase. We're watching it come to pass today. In the midst of Chapter 12, in Revelation when it says, "Woe to those that are in the earth," it helps me understand that everything won't be easy.

Now, it's a season, and we have been warned ahead of time, so we shouldn't be frightened, or ill-prepared, or surprised. In the fall, the leaves on the trees turn colors, and then after the first rainstorm the leaves fall to the ground. When that happens, don't go out in the yard and panic. It's not the end of life on planet Earth as you have known it. It's just a change of seasons. Simultaneously, the temperature will begin to drop, and the vegetation will stop growing. If you had never experienced fall or winter, it would be terrifying. If your first visit to planet Earth meant you arrived in Middle Tennessee in July, and you saw the abundant vegetation, and the humidity, and the rain, October and November would freak you out. You'd think the world was dying, and in January, there'd be no hope. But they are seasons, and you and I know they change. So, when I read that verse: "Woe to those that are in the earth," it's not a point of panic. It's a recognition there is a season coming that is going to be arduous. Get ready.

I would submit we have a responsibility—a response that we can put forward as God's people. And I chose a familiar verse, because I think it's the most direct route between here and there. The question we've been asking is, "What would God say to America?" I don't think He would say, "Do more of what you're doing." Is that fair? It seems to me we have turned our back on much of our heritage—the values that have shaped us and brought strength, abundance, prosperity, and liberty. And I am not pointing at anybody else. The Church is responsible for being the conscience of the culture. We are to be salt and light. Therefore, if darkness is gaining in intensity, it's because the light has been diminished. So, I think the responsibility begins with us, but in 2 Chronicles, we're given a remedy and a resolution from God in His message to the people:

"When I shut up the heavens so that there is no rain, or command locusts to devour the land or send a plague among my people..."

2 CHRONICLES 7:13

Do you have a notion that God gives those kinds of instructions—no rain and economic failure? That's what no rain would bring to Israel. Do you think that God might initiate sending locusts to devour, before your very eyes, every crop you had anticipated, or that He might send a plague?

"...if my people, who are called by my name, will humble themselves and pray and seek my face and turn from their wicked ways, then will I hear from heaven, and will forgive their sin and will heal their land."

2 CHRONICLES 7:14

Now, God says He'll do three things: He said He's willing to hear from Heaven, forgive our sin, and heal our land. That's a pretty amazing promise, but it's a conditional promise. We talked about those earlier, and our conditions are clearly articulated. There are four components: We have to humble ourselves, pray, seek the face of God, and turn from our wicked ways. We don't have to tell the wicked to turn. We have to turn. We're the people of God, and that responsibility lies with us.

We have been casual. We have given our hearts to idolatry—not to images carved of stone and wood or cast from metal, but we have given first priority in our lives to something other than the things of God. We've given God a casual nod. We have wanted to be included generally in the group of people that identify themselves to be Christians, but we really haven't given God first place. We haven't given Him our best thoughts and our best effort.

You know, years ago, I was a college student and making some attempt to orient my life towards God. I knew I was supposed to read my Bible, so I decided I'd begin every morning by reading Scripture. Noble thought, wasn't it? Well, as college students, we didn't believe in "early to bed, early to rise." I was getting to bed way too late and getting up early every morning to read my Bible. And every morning, I was doing the same thing—going to sleep reading my Bible—but I felt better about myself for a few weeks because I was trying to read it. Then, it occurred to me one day that it was insanity—I would read the same verse twelve times and wouldn't know what I had read. What's more, I didn't seem to be changing my sleep habit, to get to sleep earlier. Now, at that point, my primary assignment was studying. I had to use my time to learn as much as I could for grades that would pave the pathway toward a better future for me. So, I finally made a decision. I said, "God, I will give You the most productive time of my day—the time of day, Lord, when I know I am the most alert and receptive and can do my best to retain information. Lord, I'll take that block of time and read my Bible."

It wasn't a big deal. I didn't make any announcements. We didn't have the Internet or social media to post anything. We had notecards, charcoal and clay tablets. But it changed my relationship with the Lord, and it changed my Bible. I learned a principle that has stayed with me: When it comes to the context of your faith, give God your best. Stop the con! Don't just give lip service to doing something for God, truly apply yourself in the same way you apply yourself to the other interests in your life. I haven't always gotten that right, but it certainly awakened me to that principal, and it has kept me in good stead.

If you've treated God as kind of an afterthought—I mean, you don't want to be apart from Him, you've just given your best effort to other things—tell Him that you're sorry. Change. You'll be amazed at what God will do in your life.

God has given us a pathway to forgiveness and healing, but we have to humble ourselves, pray, seek His face, and turn from our wicked ways. What I love about this path is that it puts the opportunity back to us. It doesn't empower evil or the wicked. If you're looking at the news cycle, and you're filled with frustration and consternation, do what God said. "Humble yourself, pray, seek His face, and turn from your wicked ways."

We watch the news and get heated up about the wicked. Some of you need to fast the news for a day or two. It'll help your frame of mind.

Say to God, "What is there in me that would allow darkness to become more prevalent on my watch? Help me to see. Convict me, God. I'm not aware of anything. Help me!" If we will in sincerity begin to come to the Lord, God will respond to us; He said He would. Say, "Lord, if there's anything in me that is separating me from Your best, help me." God will respond to us. The courage to believe God would make a difference in and through you is desperately needed in the Church. We've been coached toward passivity for far too long. God's people are difference makers. With all of our frailty, inconsistencies, warts, and challenges we face, God will still use us. God will use you to make a difference!

Here's an example. He's one of the judges, one of the super-heroes in the Bible. His name is Gideon. I like him, but he's a very unlikely hero. Israel's adversarial opponents in Gideon's day were the Midianites, and they would come into Israel every year at harvest time and plunder the land. They left the people in a continuous deficit. The Israelites would do the work all year long, and then they would lose the fruit of their labor. After that's happened for a few years, you'd lose all hope and motivation. That's where we find Gideon threshing wheat from his harvest, but he's doing it in hiding. Normally, you'd thresh wheat in an open place so the wind would separate the grain from the chaff, but Gideon is threshing wheat in a wine-press. He's down in a depressed area, hiding, because he's afraid of the Midianites. Then, the angel of the Lord shows up:

When the angel of the LORD appeared to Gideon, he said,
"The LORD is with you, mighty warrior."

JUDGES 6:12

He called Gideon a "mighty warrior" while he was hiding. He's acting like a big chicken, but God sees Gideon from a completely different perspective.

Don't be afraid of a God-perspective in your life. Most of us live with such fear that God is mad at us, that if He could get His hands on us, He'd just shake the love of Jesus right out of us. Folks, I've read my Book: the people God is mad at, He gets to them. I suspect He loves you. He's invested in you, and sees who you could be if you would turn your heart to Him.

Finally, Gideon responds, and Gideon puts God over the hurdles. I mean, he puts out fleeces and takes them away and asks for affirmations. He is a reluctant convert to the purposes of God, but he's finally convinced he has a God-assignment. He's going to tear down the altars in his father's household. Now, he's not starting any brawl, he's just admitting, "We're idol worshipers in my household." He says, "I'm going to tear down the idols in that household." Watch the way he does it:

So Gideon took ten of his servants and did as the LORD told him. But because he was afraid of his family and the men of the town, he did it at night rather than in the daytime.

JUDGES 6:27

This is the God-proclaimed "mighty warrior" doing God's business at night because he's afraid to do it in the daylight. And yet, through Gideon's life, God brings about a tremendous victory and remarkable leadership to the nation of Israel. You can pursue the things of God with significant fear and anxiety in your heart. Don't wait until all that's gone, because you'll never start.

We ended the last chapter talking about the implications for the United States as it relates to events in our world, particularly concerning the nation of Israel and the Jewish people, along with the various nation state countries, like Iraq, Syria, and Lebanon that truthfully no longer exist as we knew them. What's going to emerge in those places is not clear yet, and there are many forces vying for control of them, from Russia to many other powers. What is clear is that all the forces in play have one unifying factor—they hate the nation of Israel. The awkward reality of that is, until very recent years, in the United States we had allied ourselves in many, many ways with the enemies of Israel. Probably, one of the most evident examples of this is in our having helped clear a pathway for Iran to become a nuclear power, contributing billions of dollars towards that initiative. Then, having treated Israel in some rather shabby ways, we were actively involved in trying to unseat their Prime Minister in a previous Israeli election—our nation did that. I suggested to you that because of those things, there are some implications for the United States, so I'll take just a minute with that.

1. PROMISE AND A WARNING

In Genesis 12, God made a promise to Abram that also contains a warning to others:

> *The LORD had said to Abram, "Leave your country, your people and your father's household and go to the land I will show you.*
>
> *I will make you into a great nation,*
> *and I will bless you;*
> *I will make your name great,*

and you will be a blessing.
I will bless those who bless you,
and whoever curses you I will curse;
and all peoples on earth
will be blessed through you."

GENESIS 12:1-3

At the end of the day, I'm a pretty simple guy. I grew up in a barn in Tennessee. You don't need a degree in theology to understand the language in that verse. God said, "Abraham, I'll bless those that bless you and your descendants, and I will curse those that curse you."

As I mentioned before, the one thing that the nations of the Middle East share in common is a conviction that the State of Israel shouldn't exist because, under Islamic thought, the principle is that once a piece of territory has come under Islamic authority, it should always remain under Islamic authority. Therefore, if another people group gains an ascendancy in some territory that once belonged to them, they feel they have a divine command to retake that territory. Again, David was king in Jerusalem more than 1,500 years before Muhammad was born, but it is true that at one point in history, the Muslim people occupied the territory that we know now as Israel. The Jewish people occupying the land of Israel in the midst of the Middle East is an affront to the Islamic world, and they can't make peace with that.

I want to ask you a question in the context of the verse we just read from Genesis: How has that worked for them? It seems to me, not too well. Their anger, hatred, hostility, vitriol, and their determination to see Israel annihilated and obliterated, has not brought great things to them. Consider the collapse of Iraq, Syria, Lebanon, along with the instability throughout the region, and the quality of life in so many, many ways. It's a powerful illustration that, perchance, we should pay attention to what God declared way back in the beginning chapters of Genesis: "I will bless those who bless you, and whoever curses you I will curse."

Now, that's not limited to the Muslim world or the nations of the Middle East. In Zechariah, there's a simple verse:

> *On that day, when all the nations of the earth are gathered against her* [Israel], *I will make Jerusalem an immovable rock for all the nations. And all who try to move it will injure themselves.*
>
> ZECHARIAH 12:3

That scenario is being played out before our very eyes. There is almost global agreement in the perspective that the State of Israel and the Jewish people are a nuisance to the world. And there are a number of examples throughout history that I could give you to support this. The British Empire, at the beginning of World War II, was the dominant world power. It was said that the sun never sets on the British Empire. In the unfolding of that conflict, the British nation really betrayed the Jewish people. They backed up on some promises they had made when it came time to withdraw from the Middle East. They gave the positions of authority and power, and the superior military positions, to Israel's enemies. And the British Empire declined in a most precipitous way. Was that the only factor? No, and I think it would be naïve to say so, but I believe it was clearly a contributing factor.

Now, the way Zechariah described "that day" is intriguing to me. He said, "I'll make Jerusalem an immovable rock and all who try to move it will injure themselves." Or more literally, "rupture themselves," not destroy themselves, but if you have a rupture, your days of heavy lifting are over. You may still be mobile and you still may exist, but your days of heavy lifting and great influence are over. Now, I have a concern for our nation. From the inception of the modern nation of Israel, we have been one of their greatest allies, advocates and proponents. Not that we always rubber stamp everything they do, or say that everything that the Jewish people do, or the State of Israel does, is right and correct; that's not true. The grossest sin you can find anywhere in America, you can find in the State of Israel today. It is not a perfect place. When you land in the nation of Israel, you don't hear the whir of angels' wings. I promise you. And yet, I believe what God said to Abram: If we curse them, God will curse us. And I am concerned when I watch the posture we have taken in recent decades, when we have been forcing "road maps" for peace upon them.

I mentioned before the hundreds of thousands of refugees that spilled out of the Middle East—overwhelmingly Muslim refugees, and predominantly young people—across Europe and further west into North America. It seems to me more than a bit ironic that there is no cry from the nations of the Middle East, and no attempt to accommodate them, resettle them, or repopulate them in the nations of the Middle East where they share culture, history and ideology. Yet, for the past fifty-plus decades, the Palestinian people on that little sliver of land we call the West Bank have been the issue fomenting so much anguish and global discussion because the refugees were intolerable there. It was unacceptable, and they had to be accommodated. They certainly couldn't be asked to move to another location or be resettled someplace else, and Israel has been the perpetrator of this great "evil," and has been labeled with all sorts of things, from an apartheid state to gross violators of human rights. Yet, in our recent history, there were hundreds of thousands of refugees being driven from the Middle East as a result of conflicts within the Muslim community itself. But this was met with a deafening silence. I believe what God said, and I believe we need a change of policy.

2. RESPONSIBILITY

I think we have a responsibility as Christians, as Christ-followers, towards the Jewish people. Anti-Semitism—the hatred of the Jewish people—is a very old form of hatred and bigotry. The Jewish people are an old people group, with stories that reach far back into time. The hatred of the Jewish people is not a new thing. From Shakespeare, to all sorts of other expressions in our political and literary history, anti-Semitism is unmistakable in all of our histories. Most of us in the West are blind to it. We don't know about the Russian pogroms. For example, in the Russian Orthodox Church, when there would be an epidemic—a drought, or something described as a disaster—it wasn't uncommon for the priests to go into the pulpits of their churches and say that the reason those things were happening was because of the Jewish people. Then, the soldiers would ride through the Jewish neighborhoods slaughtering the people. Did you see the movie or the play, *Fiddler on the Roof*? Are you familiar with the story? It's an expression of the persecution of the Jewish people in the land of Russia. But Russia's not unique.

The Spanish inquisition is another example. Time after time, after time in history, the Jewish people have been persecuted, and the primary incubator for that persecution has typically been the Church. It was very awkward to sit in class at Hebrew University in Jerusalem and study Jewish history with Jewish students who discover that you're a Christian. Then, at break time over a coffee or coming and going to class, they would say with sincerity, "Why have you hated us?" They were far more aware of the history than I was. I would submit to you, we're indebted to the Jewish people—that they are the vehicle of world redemption. It was through the Jewish people that we received the Law. It was through the Jewish people we have the prophets. Through them, we received the Scripture. Our Messiah is Jewish. Without the Jewish people, we have no redemption. There's even a twisted expression of theology that says God replaced the Jewish people with the Church, and that all the blessings that are pronounced upon Israel or the Jewish people simply have been moved over to the category of the Church. The reason for that rejection, we are told, is because they rejected the Messiah; they failed in their mission. The awkwardness of that statement is almost incomprehensible. The Church of Jesus Christ has existed in the earth for two millennia. Jesus gave us a very clear commission to go into all the world and preach the gospel to every person (Mark 16:15). If we're going to talk about failing in our assignments, before we point a finger at anyone else, we'd better look in the mirror.

Paul is clear in Romans chapter 9:

> ...the people of Israel. Theirs is the adoption of sons, the divine glory, the covenants, the receiving of the law, the temple worship, and the promises. Theirs are the patriarchs and from them is traced the human ancestry of Christ, who is God over

all forever praised. Amen.

ROMANS 9:4-5

Simply put, we owe a debt to the Jewish people. They have suffered for the truth they carried that we have all benefited from. Are they perfect? Hardly. Do the same sins that plague us plague them? Absolutely. Nonetheless, we are indebted to the Jewish people. At the very least, we should make it a matter of daily prayer for the peace of Jerusalem—not just an absence of conflict—but for a peace between the inhabitants of that land and the God who led them there. Doing so will change your life and mine.

3. GOD BLESS AMERICA

There's a third piece, and it's a commitment in your heart to pray that God would bless America. Your life makes a difference. Your prayers make a difference. The existence of the Church makes a difference. The ideas around which America has been organized and flourished and prospered, has made a difference in our world. I know it's not popular to say. I know you'll get more ink and more attention in the media if you'll be negative about America and talk about our weaknesses and our failures. We are a nation of people, and people come broken. In any broad collection of people, it won't be impossible or even difficult to find weaknesses and failures of character, choices, and behavior.

Nevertheless, the idea and principles around which America has been organized are unique in the earth and have brought about a unique result. We should be grateful and celebratory of them and spend ourselves preserving them for the generation that follows us. Social Security will not secure us. Only the principles of Almighty God in our midst will secure us. If we set aside God's ideas about family, morality, behavior, integrity, and truth, we will not flourish.

In Deuteronomy 30, Moses' mission is just about done, and he gives the people an assignment:

> *"This day I call heaven and earth as witnesses against you that I have set before you life and death, blessings and curses. Now choose life, so that you and your children may live and that you may love the Lord your God, listen to his voice, and hold fast to him."*

DEUTERONOMY 30:19-20

It's a choice. In the plainest of language, you and I have to desire a godly influence in our lives. We need to have a desire for godly leaders, or we will never experience the life and blessings God desires to give us. It's not enough to want godliness in some distant place, like Pennsylvania Avenue or the Halls of Congress. We have to choose godliness in the context of our homes and our family systems. It's inconsistent to want leaders at the highest levels of the land to work for righteousness when we're not willing to stand for it in our sphere of influence. If we tolerate idolatry, immorality, and ungodliness, and excuse it with a wink and a nod because it's inconvenient to do anything else, why should we imagine others would sacrifice themselves to stand for those principles in a broader way? We have to choose life.

Psalm 75 reminds us that God is the Judge; He puts down one and He exalts another (Psalm 75:7). Daniel, in chapter 2 and verse 21, presents a very similar idea: "It is he, God, who changes the times and epochs." *Epoch* is a broader span of time. "He removes kings and establishes kings. He gives wisdom to the wise men and knowledge to men of understanding." God is the one who lifts up and puts down. I've said and will continue to say that the greatest forces that are available to human beings are spiritual. Not to diminish the others, but the Church of Jesus Christ has to be awakened to that idea and cry out to God.

Finally, I would submit to you there's a cost for choosing life. I'll never forget Lance Lambert, standing in Three Crosses Sanctuary. He had lost more than forty members of his family in the Holocaust, including his father, who was an Italian Count. Lance Lambert was a remarkable man. The last time he was here was his last public meeting before he went to Heaven. Lance said then that he thought God would pour out His Spirit on America again, *if* we were willing to pay the price, and he said he didn't know if we were. He didn't say it in a haughty way, but he said it in a way I've never forgotten. I honestly don't know the answer to our willingness. I do believe God is willing, I'm not sure we are. I think we're grappling with it and trying to understand the cost.

In Philippians, Paul said:

Whatever was to my profit, I now consider loss for the sake of Christ. And what is more, I consider everything a loss compared to the surpassing greatness of knowing Christ Jesus, my Lord for whose sake I have lost all things.

PHILIPPIANS 3:7-8

I don't believe that's just rhetoric. Paul left a very promising career. He left a whole set of friends. He set aside a whole set of authority. He became an itinerant traveler around the Mediterranean world. And if you know his story, it seemed everywhere he went, there was a riot, or an imprisonment, or some sort of physical challenge that he faced. Yet, from his efforts, the world of his day was changed. I believe it began with that attitude in his heart. He said, "I have lost all things for Christ!"

In Jude 1—I bet you don't read Jude a lot—it says:

Dear friends, although I was eager to write to you about the salvation we share, I felt I had to write and urge you to contend for the faith that was once for all entrusted to the saints.

JUDE 1:3

Do you have that idea? You see, I think we're kind of offended that evil would dare present itself. Yet, the language Paul uses here is that we have to "contend for the faith." You'll do it in your home. You'll do it in the marketplace. We'll do it in the school systems. We will do it in the public arena. There is a contentiousness in all these places. Remember who we looked at back in Revelation 12? There's an adversary to the purposes of God in the earth. If there was a war in Heaven, what do you think we're going to have on earth? A dress rehearsal? A pre-season game, where the first team only plays for a few minutes and then we go sit on the sidelines?

In 2 Timothy, chapter 2 and verse 3, Paul mentored Timothy: "Endure hardship with us like a good soldier of Christ Jesus." He didn't say, "Timothy, I've borne all the hardships so you don't have to." We've been a little guilty of not wanting the generations coming behind us to bear anything. It won't work, and we'll rob them of what God created them for. Endure hardship. Folks, don't be afraid of what's ahead. Stand up and say, "Lord, prepare me. Holy Spirit, begin to prepare me, and give me the insight I need. Help me to understand the authority You've invested in me. If there's any harmful thing in me, help me to see it. If I have tolerated anything that diminishes or limits what You created me for, help me to see it. I'll turn away from it." God has called us to this season. Just as certainly as God called David to the season he was in, along with the mighty men with him in the desert near Ein Gedi, He's called you and me to this season. Just as certainly as He called Washington and Jefferson and Adams, He's called us to this season.

Now, what will be said of us? We saw the conflict, and we went and hid in our tents? I don't want that to be my story. Would I prefer that evil just yield, and we could sing "Amazing Grace" while we walk down the street? Probably, but it's not realistic. So let's tell the Lord we want to go through. Let's take the invitation of the 2 Chronicles passage to heart and humble ourselves, and pray, and seek the face of God, and be willing to turn from our own ungodliness instead of pointing the finger at someone else. Then, let's watch what God will do. Amen? Make this your prayer:

Father, thank You for Your Word, for its truth, authority, and power. I thank You for Your Church in the earth, Lord. It's a point of tremendous hope. I thank You that You have given us authority—that we don't just sing songs and convene studies, but we're the people of Almighty God on planet Earth at this unique season in time. And Lord, I come in humility. We are a nation in need of healing. We have consumed Your blessings and at the same time been ungrateful, and I ask for Your mercy and Your forgiveness.

Lord, I turn my face to You. Holy Spirit, I give You permission

to search my heart. If there's anything in me that separates me from God's best, I pray that You will convict me, Lord, that I won't be content or satisfied, that I won't be able to push it aside or be distracted, that I will become so aware that I will come in humility, and repentance, to turn away. I thank You, Lord.

I pray that You will give us leaders—from the lowest levels in the land to the highest—men and women who fear Your Name; men and women who will have the courage to stand for truth and righteousness. Lord, I offer myself as a living sacrifice, laying aside anything that entangles or hinders me from giving You my very best. Thank You for what You will do, that You will bring me through triumphantly as more than an overcomer. In Jesus' name, amen.

GOD BLESS AMERICA AGAIN

INTO THE ARENA

I. GOD'S PERSPECTIVE

I would submit to you that we desperately need a prophetic perspective on twenty-first century American life—not our opinion, not our feelings—God's perspective. Too much of our prayer lives, too much of our relationship with God, has been an effort to try to get God to understand our perspective: "God, don't You know how I feel? Don't you know my circumstances? Aren't you aware of the people and the things that are putting pressure on me?" Not inappropriate prayers, but if they're the only prayers we pray, our lives are void of a very important component, and that is knowing what God has to say about who we are and how we're conducting ourselves and our circumstances.

So we've entitled this study *God Bless America*, because I have a desire to see God pour His blessings out upon our nation. It's important, so what I'm suggesting is we need to begin with a

God-perspective in our hearts, and our lives, and our homes, and our nation. If we will do that, we can trust God to respond.

A. ALL SUFFICIENT

I want to start with some things that would simply serve us well to keep in mind. I think one of the ways that the evil one limits the effectiveness of God's people is he gets us engaged in peripheral issues. We will argue about the color of the grape juice with which we serve communion, or the translation of the Bible we read, or what time we worship—things that may have some impact upon our faith, but they are, at best, secondary issues. And there are some things I would submit that we can't afford to lose sight of. The first one is that God is all-sufficient. The God we worship is almighty and all-sufficient. What that means, in the plainest of language, is He doesn't need anything from us. I have nothing that will improve the quality of God's existence. He is completely sufficient apart from me. That's good to know.

Look at Psalm, chapter 2:

Why do the nations conspire and the peoples plot in vain? The kings of the earth take their stand and the rulers gather together against the LORD and against his Anointed One. "Let us break their chains," they say, "and throw off their fetters." The One enthroned in heaven laughs; the Lord scoffs

at them. Then he rebukes them in his anger and terrifies them
in his wrath, saying, "I have installed my King on Zion, my
holy hill."

PSALM 2:1-6

This verse begins with a rhetorical question, but it's important to know the question was asked more than 1,000 years before the birth of Jesus. I think twenty-first century Christians want to imagine that now is the first time in the history of humanity that there have been sophisticated organizations rebelling against God. It is the nature of human beings to rebel against God. It's been our story from the Garden until today. These rulers of the earth say, "We don't intend to be fettered or limited by a God-perspective. We don't want God's boundaries to be our boundaries. We don't want God's requirements to be our requirements." So, they gathered together with plots and schemes to separate themselves from a God-perspective, and then the psalmist gives us God's response: God looks at the plots, wickedness, and the rebellion of human beings, and it says that He's amused. Why? Because He isn't threatened. He isn't intimidated. We have nothing with which to threaten Him. He is all-sufficient. That's our God. It's why we worship Him.

You see, we've reduced God to an expression of a worship service or a denomination or a congregational affiliation. Those are not evil things, but the God we worship is far beyond those things. He's the Creator of Heaven and Earth and everything that's in them. Everything that exists is held together by His authority and His power. It's why we worship Him. He is worthy to be worshipped. Worship isn't because God's ego is so fragile He needs to be reminded that He's really swell. Worship is because we lose perspective. We need to gather with like-minded people to lift our hearts and our voices to God, and to remember that there is a God who sustains our lives, and that He is all-sufficient. I love what God says in Psalm 50. God said:

> *"I have no need of a bull from your stall or of goats from your pens, for every animal of the forest is mine, and the cattle on a thousand hills. I know every bird in the mountains, and the insects in the fields are mine. If I were hungry I would not tell you, for the world is mine, and all that is in it."*

PSALM 50:9-12

It makes me smile. God said, "Look, folks, if I needed something, I'm not ringing your phone. I'm not going to hit you with a text, because you don't have anything that would help Me." He said, "When I think of you, it's a liability." And yet, He loves us. Our God is all-sufficient.

B. A DELIVERER

There's a second perspective of God I would encourage you to hold in your heart, and it's that our God is a God who delivers.

Inexplicably (Scripture really doesn't offer us an explanation), God has chosen to intervene on behalf of humanity, no matter how persistently rebellious we have been, to bring deliverance to our lives. The Bible tells us that the Jesus-story is the ultimate expression of that—the Incarnation—that God's Son became one of us to redeem us. Our God is a delivering God. He desires, He's interested, He's willing—it is His mode of operation on our behalf, in spite of our stubbornness. Our God is a deliverer. In 2 Chronicles, there's a marvelous verse. The king's name is Asa. The specifics are not overly significant, other than there's an army threatening the nation, and Asa makes a declaration of faith that speaks to us through the centuries:

> *"LORD, there is no one like you to help the powerless against the mighty. Help us, O LORD our God, for we rely on you, and in your name we have come against this vast army. O LORD, you are our God; do not let man prevail against you."*

> 2 CHRONICLES 14:11

If you're not in the habit of praying the scriptures, I commend it to you. That's a marvelous one-verse prayer for your life when you face challenges that you feel powerless to overcome. They come to all of our lives. They come in the form of a medical diagnosis. They come in the form of a relational challenge, a financial need. They come in many, many ways. Life is more difficult than I would wish. Have you noticed? For good people, not just for wicked people, or immoral people—for people doing the best they know to do. Life is often very challenging. These words are so helpful: "There is no one like You to help the powerless against the mighty. Help us—we rely on You. In Your name we have come against this vast opposing force. Don't let man prevail against You, God." Our God is a deliverer.

Daniel is a marvelous book in the Hebrew Bible. Daniel is a hero. It's a book filled with heroes. Daniel lived in a difficult season. He's a foreign slave in the land of Babylon. Jerusalem's destroyed, and there are many stories included in that book about the triumph of God in the life of somebody in the most dire circumstances. But we're introduced to three of Daniel's friends—three young men, his contemporaries. They've got big names: Shadrach, Meshach, and Abednego. You know, call them Paul, Ringo, and John if it helps you. The king of Babylon decides that he's going to build a statue of himself. King Nebuchadnezzar has a bit of an ego issue. You'll enjoy reading the book because God speaks to his ego. God says, in just good old country language, "Dude, you're a little puffed up." You'll have to read the book to find out what God does to him, but he levels the field. But at this season, Nebuchadnezzar is still pretty full of himself, so he builds the statue, and the edict is given that everybody will have to bow down to the statue. And at the appointed time, everybody bows down except these three young men. There they stand rather prominent in their disobedience, and the king is so shocked that anybody would challenge his order that he wants to meet the three with the audacity to stand when it's time to bow. So, they have an appointment with the king.

Now, I want to remind you of something. These three young men have had a horrific set of life-circumstances. They are slaves in a foreign country. Their nation has been destroyed. Their peer group, for the most part, has been slaughtered. They have every reason to have lives that are torqued with anger, resentment, bitterness, and hatred—even towards God. You see, life isn't going their way. There isn't momentum. Their dreams have been totally shredded. Their parents' ambitions for them are dust that's been blown away in the wind. They have every reason to have hard hearts and be warped, and yet, they're not. You see, one of the challenges that I want to give to the American Church is this—we have looked for too many excuses to justify our ungodliness: "Well, my family system wasn't just right. I didn't get to go to the school I wanted to. I was not treated appropriately in some context." All of those things can be true and very painful, but they're not legitimate reasons to rebel against God. We have looked for license more than we have looked for integrity. Listen to how Shadrach, Meshach, and Abednego respond to the king:

"O Nebuchadnezzar, we do not need to defend ourselves before you in this matter. If we are thrown into the blazing furnace, the God we serve is able to save us from it, and he

will rescue us from your hand, O king. But even if he does not,
we want you to know, O king, that we will not serve your
gods or worship the image of gold you have set up."

DANIEL 3:16-18

You've got to love their courage: "We worship a God that's more powerful than you. You've got a statue, but our God is more powerful than your statue, and He'll deliver us." But the next statement is even more remarkable: "Our God is more powerful than you, and He can deliver us. But let's be clear, king, if He doesn't, we're still not going to bow." That is not a politically correct statement. If we were going to conduct that discussion in the public square today, it would sound very different, wouldn't it? We'd say, "Well, Nebuchadnezzar, we appreciate the authority with which you rule and the diversity of your empire. You have gathered people from the nations of the world." And in our politically correct, warped perspective, we would find some way to justify kneeling.

Folks, our God is a deliverer. He delivers from sickness and disease. He delivers us from the bondage of sin and habits. Our God is faithful. We need that tucked in our heart. It's more than church services we conduct or polite little social classes on ethics. We worship an Almighty God, who intervenes in the earth on behalf of His people.

C. AWARE—"WELL DONE"

There's one more piece I would give you; our God is aware. He's paying attention. It's expressed in so many ways in the Bible. Jesus told a parable about a wealthy landowner who was leaving for an extended period, and he gathered some of his most trusted workers together and gave to them significant blocks of his resources. After a long time, he returns and he asks for an accounting. Many of you know it as the "Parable of the Talents." I'll just give you one verse from that story Jesus told us:

> *"His master replied, 'Well done, good and faithful servant! You have been faithful with a few things; I will put you in charge of many things. Come and share your master's happiness!'"*

MATTHEW 25:21

The principle is very simple: If you're faithful in a few small things, you can be entrusted with things of much more significance. But to be entrusted with things of significance or great value, first, you have to prove yourself faithful in the small, overlooked, insignificant things. At the heart of that is this idea that God is aware. It was a central part of Jesus' message. He said to His audience on more than one occasion: "Don't you know God watches over your lives? If a sparrow falls to the ground, God takes note of that" (Matthew 10:29). Scripture says that God pays attention to the flowers in the field, and He sees to it that they're clothed with beauty (Matthew 6:28-30). And

Jesus said, "You're a lot more valuable than a bird or a flower. God will tend to you. He knows that you need food to eat and shelter and clothing, and He'll care for that if you will seek Him first" (Matthew 6:31-33). He said, "God knows how many hairs you have on your head" (Luke 12:7). For some of us, that's not a huge calculation. But it's not just a Jesus-message. It's part of the tone of Scripture.

In Deuteronomy 28, where the blessings of Abraham are delineated, it says that God will bless you "when you sit and when you stand" (verse 6). That's more than just rhetoric. It says God will "bless you in the city and in the field" (verse 3). That doesn't mean God will bless the urbanites and the rural folk. It means God is watching over our lives—He knows where we are, that His blessings are associated with our lives. God is aware of our lives. People who lead deceptive lives, manipulative lives, hold an imagination that God can be mocked—that they have outsmarted Him. I would, just in passing, give you the reminder that every one of us has an appointment with Almighty God. Don't carry unforgiveness in your heart for deceptive people. Don't carry anger and resentment for people that seem to be getting away with evil. I can assure you, there's no getting away. They have an appointment, and justice is coming. You honor the Lord. It's the reason Jesus said to pray for those who do all manner of evil against you. He said that when they mistreat you and speak ill of you, to rejoice. That's irrational. It's illogical. You know why He said it? He basically said, "There's a great reward for you. They're living on a very limited plane with a very limited perspective. So, when you encounter injustice, don't ball your fist in rage. Raise your hands in worship to Almighty God. There's a great reward coming for you" (Matthew 5:11-12). The God we worship, the all-sufficient One, the God Who's a deliverer, is aware of our lives, and they don't go untended. What a marvelous promise.

II. WHICH SIDE?

I want to take a moment with you and look at a chapter from the book of Isaiah. It's Isaiah 59; it's a marvelous chapter in Scripture. I've just taken some slices from the chapter, but if you want to do a little extra work on your own, read Isaiah 59 this week. Think about what the prophet has to say. The message is very simple. The thesis is illustrated—clearly stated, in the first verse: "Surely the arm of the LORD is not too short to save, nor his ear too dull to hear." What a marvelous promise. God said, "My arm's not too short and My strength's not insufficient, and I can hear you. I can get to you, and I can hear your problem." Isn't that good to know? That's my God. I mean, He can be yours, too, but I can tell you for sure, He's mine. God desires to bring freedom to His people.

That's so good to know, but look at verse 2:

"But your iniquities have separated you from your God; your

sins have hidden his face from you, so that he will not hear.
For your hands are stained with blood, your fingers with
guilt. Your lips have spoken lies, and your tongue mutters
wicked things. No one calls for justice; no one pleads his case
with integrity. They rely on empty arguments and speak lies;
they conceive trouble and give birth to evil."

ISAIAH 59:2-4

It sounds like a pretty accurate description of contemporary American life. What happened? God said that His strength is sufficient. His reach is adequate. His awareness is complete. How have we arrived at this condition? It says that our iniquities have brought the separation. God hasn't withdrawn from us; our iniquities—the attitude of our heart, our choices, our thoughts, our values—have brought separation between ourselves and God. Now, there's good news in that; if our choices have brought the separation, that separation can be bridged. It's not something done to us. This is a passage written to the people of God—to God's covenant people, His chosen people—not the pagan nations. Look in verse 13:

...rebellion and treachery against the LORD, turning our
backs on our God, fomenting oppression and revolt, uttering
lies our hearts have conceived. So justice is driven back, and
righteousness stands at a distance; truth has stumbled in the
streets, honesty cannot enter. Truth is nowhere to be found,

and whoever shuns evil becomes a prey. The LORD looked
and was displeased that there was no justice.

ISAIAH 59:13-15

Again, it sounds very descriptive of our world, doesn't it? Truth is nowhere to be found and if you shun evil, you're mocked. If you choose to live a biblically informed life—if you choose a biblically informed sexuality, or morality, or do business in an ethical way—far too frequently you're mocked, made fun of, seen as somehow unsophisticated. Verse 14 intrigues me. There are four words used: *justice*, *righteousness*, *truth*, and *honesty*. How many of you think the quality of your life would improve if there was a significant growth in those four things—justice, righteousness, truth, and honesty? Me, too. I happen to think those are words of great significance. They're important words. Those words don't exist apart from the power of God. Those words are not achievable or attainable apart from God, because the human condition does not lend itself to justice, righteousness, honesty, and truth apart from God. There's nothing in the history of human civilization that suggests human beings working together will arrive at a place of justice, righteousness, truth, and honesty, unless there's an intervention, because we are a rebellious lot. We look for opportunities and advantages. We are filled with selfishness, selfish ambition, envy, greed, and immorality. We need the intervention of the power of God. Our story is a story of transformation, whereby the power of a living

God results in the transformation of a human life, so that we can live together in justice, and honesty, and righteousness, and truth. It's what makes the cross—the gospel story—good news. The good news is that, through the power of the cross, we can be changed and live together in a way that enables us all to flourish. It's a myth that a government, or a leader, or anyone else, or any organization, apart from the power of the gospel, can achieve that outcome. There's no evidence of it in human history. Don't be ashamed because you're a person of faith. Don't be ashamed to say, "My faith needs to impact the office where I work, or the neighborhood where I live, or the school where I teach, or where my children attend, or the ballfields where my children interact." Your faith—those values, and the transformation that has been initiated in your heart and mine—is the hope that we hold. It's important. We've been timid too long, folks. We're not getting better apart from God. We're not treating one another with greater dignity, and greater unity, and greater cooperation, apart from God.

Look at those words again in verse 14: *justice, righteousness, truth,* and *honesty.* There's a statement made about each one of them. Justice, it says, "is driven back." Righteousness "stands at a distance." Truth has "stumbled," and honesty isn't even allowed to "enter." Sounds pretty descriptive, doesn't it? What intrigues me is every one of those descriptions addresses proximity or availability. Righteousness stands at a distance. Justice is driven back. Truth has stumbled. Honesty isn't allowed to enter. They're not close enough; they're not available. We need the promise of verse 1, that "the arm of the Lord is not too short, nor His ears to dull to hear."

How have we arrived at this position? The iniquity of our hearts. Look at verse 19:

From the west, men will fear the name of the LORD, and from the rising of the sun, they will revere his glory.

ISAIAH 59:19

That's a fascinating passage. The first phrase resonates in my heart: "From the west," it says, "men will fear the name of the Lord." From the perspective of the authors of Scripture, who were from the Middle East, "the west" is us—America. It says, "From the west will come the fear of the Lord." I began to say it as if it was God's perspective over our lives: "God, let the reverence for God—a respect for God, the fear of God—come once again from the West. Let the western peoples fear the name of the Lord. Let it be true over our lives, God." There was a time we were known as the Christian West. Many would like to take that label away from us. I would like us to be known as a generation that fears the name of the Lord. Let it sweep around the earth. Now in fairness to the text, look at the next phrase: "... from the rising of the sun, they will revere his glory." Where does the sun rise? The East. So, from the west to the east—let the whole earth be filled with a reverence for God. It's an equal and balanced understanding of the passage, but I'm not giving up the fear of the Lord coming from the West. Look at verse 20: "The Redeemer will come to Zion, to those in Jacob who repent of their sins …" That's the punch line: The Redeemer will come to those who "repent of their sins." Go back to the first verse where Isaiah said, "Surely the arm of the LORD is not too short to save, nor his ear too dull to hear." And now, verse 20 again, "the Redeemer will come" to those "who repent."

What has caused the gulf? What's caused justice, righteousness, truth, and honesty to be removed from our proximity? It's been the iniquities of our own heart. We're not powerless; we can change. What would God say to America? What do you think He would say to us if He occupied our pulpits? I think He would ask us about the thousands of children that we sacrifice each day because it's inconvenient or too economically challenging. I think He would ask us about the more than 50,000,000 babies we have lost since Roe v. Wade. Oh, I know we have to have compassion on people that have endured abortions. I'm an advocate for that, but I think God would ask us about this issue. We get way torqued up about justice, folks, and our rights, and thousands of children every week lose their lives with no voice in the public square. I think God would talk to us about that. I think God would talk to us about the casual way we have set aside His moral boundaries, and we've chosen our own.

I think He would talk about the lack of contentment in our hearts. I sit with pastors frequently, and I often have the privilege of sitting with pastors that have been very effective in leading large and even global ministries, churches, and initiatives— remarkable people in many ways. But I'm concerned. It's easy to convene one of those meetings and share our stories and point at the things that we have accomplished, yet miss the bigger picture.

World Outreach Church is the place I know God has planted me for this season, and our church is a remarkable expression in many ways of the grace of God. When I became a part of it many years ago, we were in a little rented space. Then, we bought some property. Our first worship services, here, were in a tent, and it was more beautiful to us than Solomon's Temple. Now, many years later, the Lord has blessed us in phenomenal ways, but you know the greater reality? The percentage of our community that participates in church is the lowest it has ever been. In Murfreesboro, and in Rutherford County, the buckle of the Bible Belt, fewer people participate in worship on a weekend than in the history of this city or this county. I don't think I can stand before the Lord and point at what we've done and say, "Wow." In the future, I hope we have to have church on Tuesday afternoons to accommodate the people who want to come worship.

III. PREPARATION, FOR THOSE LISTENING

Now, I want to look with you at a passage that I believe the Lord gave us for how to be prepared for what is yet ahead. It's an important question, "how do we prepare?" It's an important life-question. I was talking to a family between services one day that had a new baby. We talked about the changes the baby had brought to their lives. You can't help but smile—you spend months and months preparing, and the baby gets here and you feel completely unprepared. "Why didn't somebody tell us?" Because you can't quite hear until that first one arrives, right? Preparation is important. When we change seasons from summer to fall, there's that first hint of cool in the early morning, and we know to anticipate the season ahead.

We have to care and listen. Preparation is only effective for those who are listening. I happen to believe that before the Lord comes we'll see the greatest harvest into the Kingdom of God that the world has ever seen. Before you applaud that in your heart, understand that harvest time is a time of incredibly hard work. Harvest time is a time of extraordinary effort and tremendous diligence. If you don't participate in the harvest—if you sleep through the harvest, or you choose to vacation during the harvest—you forfeit what's needed for the leaner season that is to come.

Years ago, when we were still living at home, we planted a strawberry patch. We liked fresh strawberries. Our parents humored us and helped us with the strawberry patch, and the first year was kind of nice. It was manageable. Strawberries grew. Two or three years into it, we had what felt like a 40-acre field of strawberries. It was probably about a half an acre. Now, it was fun that first time you got to pick those strawberries. I liked fresh strawberries, particularly if somebody will wash them and cap them, put a little sugar on them, make some shortbread, and put it all in a bowl in front of me with some whipped cream. I'm all about that. That's a God-thing. I was willing to pick, you know, a row of strawberries to get to that objective the first time. But those plants kept bearing, and my parents had this perverse notion that we should pick strawberries to share with our friends. Ugh—if they want strawberries, let them come pick their own strawberries. About 10 days into strawberry season, I hated strawberries. I didn't like my friends. They were enjoying the good life from the sweat of my brow.

I grew up in the country, and we used to have a field of hay. We would cut hay, and we'd fertilize and sow seed in that field, because we knew when the grass stopped growing we still needed to feed the livestock. So, we'd cut hay—not like we do it today. Now, folks cut hay and put it into big round bales and move it with fancy hydraulic equipment. We used to cut hay and put it in these little evil blocks and make our children move it. That was harvest time. There was abundance. There was so much abundance we couldn't consume it all. We would gather it, collect it, stack it, and store it, because we were going to need it for another season.

Folks, its harvest time. That doesn't mean it's easy. It's not a vacation. It's not a day at the park. You're going to need gloves. You're going to get tired. But it's a season that has a terminal point on it, and if we don't respond to the season, we'll forfeit the opportunity. In Ephesians, we're given a passage that helps us prepare:

Finally, be strong in the Lord and in his mighty power. Put on the full armor of God, so that you can take your stand against the devil's schemes. For our struggle is not against flesh and blood, but against the rulers, against the authorities, against the powers of this dark world and against the spiritual forces of evil in the heavenly realms. Therefore put on the full armor of God, so that when the day of evil comes, you may be able to stand your ground, and after you have done everything, to stand. Stand firm then, with the belt of truth buckled around your waist, with the breastplate of righteousness in place, and with your feet fitted with the readiness that comes from the

gospel of peace. In addition to all this, take up the shield of
faith, with which you can extinguish all the flaming arrows
of the evil one. Take the helmet of salvation and the sword
of the Spirit, which is the word of God. And pray in the
Spirit on all occasions with all kinds of prayers and requests.
With this in mind, be alert and always keep on praying for
all the saints.

EPHESIAN 6:10-18

It's not a complex passage; the language is very accessible, and twice in the first three verses we are given the counsel to "put on the full armor of God." The following is a quick delineation of this set of verses.

A. STRONG IN THE LORD & HIS MIGHTY POWER

First of all, it says in verse 10: "Be strong in the Lord and in his mighty power." It's not presented to us as an option. If we're going to walk through this season effectively, you and I will have to be strong in the Lord and in His power. You say, "Now, wait a minute, Pastor. I just come to church. Look, there may be a hell, and I don't want to go there. It's really all I want. I want to get my ticket punched for heaven, and then I'm going to leave the heavy lifting to the rest of you goofballs." You won't make it. I doubt you'll even make heaven. You see, the idea that you can recite a prayer, be dunked in a pool, and then live your life on your terms for your goals, while ignoring the purposes of God, and still receive the benefit of the people of God is a very frightening notion to me. It's not one I'm willing to bet my eternity on. I'm not talking about being a preacher. When Jesus gave us a prayer, He's told us to pray it on a daily basis: "Let Your will be done and Your Kingdom come through me" (Matthew 6:10). We are learning to be strong in the Lord.

B. PUT ON THE FULL ARMOR OF GOD... ENABLED TO STAND

We're told in verse 11: "Put on the full armor of God ..." It's repeated again in verse 13. Why would you put on the armor God? Because it's such a fashion statement? No, it says to put on the full armor of God so that you'll be able to stand. If you don't have on the armor, you won't stand. You won't make it. I believe that with all my heart. We need the armor. That's why it's given to us, and there are seven specific components that are enumerated there:

1. **Belt of Truth around Your Waist:** It says to put the belt of truth around your waist. If you don't choose the truth for your life—the truth about yourself, the truth for yourself— if you aren't a person of the truth; you can't even keep your pants up. It's really hard to walk when they keep falling down. It's embarrassing and humiliating. You need truth.

2. **Breastplate of Righteousness**

3. **Feet Fitted With Readiness from Gospel of Peace**

4. **Take up the Shield of Faith:** To extinguish all flaming arrows of the evil one, you take up the shield of faith. You have to choose to take it up. It's available, but you have to choose it. Why would you choose it? Because there are fiery darts launched by something evil at your life, and you can't extinguish them without faith.

5. **Helmet of Salvation:** The helmet of salvation protects your mind. There's a battle in our minds—in all of our minds. The battle is not just with evil thoughts, or illicit thoughts, or immoral thoughts—there are battles in our mind about forgiveness and the pathway that God's inviting us toward.

6. **Sword of Spirit, Word of God:** We need God's Word to help us—the sword of the Spirit, the Word of God.

7. **Pray in The Spirit:** Finally, pray in the Spirit on all occasions with all kinds of prayers.

C. KNOW THE ADVERSARY

We get the rest of the instructions on how to prepare for the harvest in verse 12, where it says to know your adversary. It says, "For our struggle is not against flesh and blood ..." Do you know why it says that? Because at first glance, it looks like most of my problems are with people. The people may not be my problem, but they're the delivery system. And Paul is reminding us that our wrestling match, our struggle, really isn't with people. It's with principalities and powers and spiritual forces of wickedness in the heavenly places. There's a spiritual motivation for evil. "Well, I don't know if I believe that or not, Pastor." That's why we're looking at this—it's in the Book. Spiritual forces of evil are not some secondary component; they are the fundamental force behind the challenges we face.

D. DAY OF EVIL COMES

In verse 13, it tells us the next component: "Therefore put on the full armor of God, so that when the day of evil comes..." We've been warned. Something's going to arrive in your life that could only legitimately be described as evil. You didn't invite it. You didn't want it. You didn't earn it. You didn't deserve it. It just intruded. Jesus said to the disciples, "When we get to Jerusalem, this is what's going to happen." Were they prepared? Not very well. After the fact, they recalled that they had been warned.

E. HAVING DONE EVERYTHING— STAND

In verse 13, we get some more instructions: "So that when the day of evil comes, you may be able to stand your ground, and after you have done everything, to stand. Stand firm then."

Sometimes you'll have done everything you know to do. You'll have prayed every prayer. You'll have responded with every response. You will have done everything you've known to do, and you don't have the resolution you need yet. What do you do then? You stand. It feels a lot to me like perseverance or endurance.

F. BE ALERT

In verse 18, it says: "With this in mind, be alert …" It's going to require awareness on our parts. Be alert.

G. ALWAYS KEEP ON PRAYING FOR ALL THE SAINTS

Finally, in the last part of verse 18, it says: "Always keep on praying for all the saints." You know why we're told to keep on praying? Because we get tired of praying for the saints. I'm thinking, *Saints, pray for yourself. How much prayer do I have to make for the saints? It seems to me there are more ain'ts than there are saints. Let somebody else pray for a while.* But it says we have to keep on praying for all the saints.

We live in a very unique season. God is moving in the earth in an unprecedented way. I believe the years ahead of us hold the potential for the greatest move of the Spirit of God that humanity will have ever known, but I also believe they hold the potential for the greatest expressions of evil our world will have ever seen. The question is whether or not we'll be prepared for that season. It's not helpful to lament the fact that the season is changing. Folks, you can be upset because summer is about over, but it won't keep the fall and the winter from coming. I meet people who lament that we're not in some season and some previous place. Okay, I hear you. Maybe I regret that with you, but we've got a future to face. Let's go. God has given you everything the Bible says you need for life and godliness (2 Peter 1:3). His arm is not too short, His strength isn't too small, and His hearing is not too dull (Isaiah 59:1), and He will come for His people (Revelation 22:12). I want to be included in that group, don't you? Amen.

Pray this prayer:

Heavenly Father, I come to you because in You there is hope. You are a God of great mercy and compassion, a God who restores and renews. As a nation, we are in great need. We have turned our backs on truth and justice. We have walked in pride and rebellion. Forgive our sins, and pour out upon us a spirit of humility and repentance. May the fear of God wash over our hearts and our minds. Our hope is in the name of our Lord. May Jesus be honored in this generation. Amen.

GOD BLESS AMERICA AGAIN

WHAT SHOULD WE DO?

I want to try to answer a question, at least in part: What is it exactly we should do? You know, I've talked to lots of people, and I interact with many Christians across all of our different stations, places, and backgrounds, and this is almost the same question they put to me. There is a sense of futility right now. Beyond the fear, the chaos, the anxiety, the stress, and all the division in our nation, and all the things that we can see that are inappropriate and that need to be addressed and changed; the thing I hear most is a sense of feeling impotent, of powerlessness. What do I do in the face of this? I'm just one person. We're inundated with messages from the healthcare community and public health officials, the scientific community, the economists, the political scientists, and all the prognosticators and pollsters. It's like a tsunami of bad news that just washes over us every day, and the thing that is missing in the midst of that, I believe, is the response of the Church.

We have a role to play. And I believe the reason, for the most part, that we have been silent, or are willing to go home and be quiet and content with the live stream, is we didn't understand the authority that had been invested in us. We have a role to play, and we are just as mission-critical to walking out of this season of confusion, chaos, and plague, as any healthcare provider, or any political leader. If the Church fails in our responsibility, the confusion, chaos and anarchy will increase.

We have spiritual tools—knowing the Word of God so that we know the character of God; being people of prayer; standing in the name of Jesus and in the authority of Jesus' blood. Those tools change the course of human history, and their delivery system is the Church of Jesus Christ. It's not about the label of the church where you worship, or the denomination you prefer, or the musical style that suits your own personal taste, or the architecture that is most pleasing to you aesthetically. All of those things may have some place, but they are not of primary importance. We stand under the headship of Jesus of Nazareth. We're His Body. We're placed on this Earth on an assignment, and it's not personally driven; it's not selfishly motivated.

I. THE INFLUENCE OF CHRISTIANITY UPON OUR NATION

I want to start for just a minute with the influence of Christianity upon our nation. Unfortunately, the history that I learned in school is seldom taught these days. I can tell you this: Christianity has been the single most profound influence in shaping the values, the course, and the direction of our nation. I believe that because of our faith, we have been uniquely blessed by God. I've had the privilege of traveling a bit around the world, and I can tell you that the nations of the world do not enjoy the liberties and the freedoms, the abundance, and the opportunities that we take for granted. If it were universal in scope, there wouldn't be millions of people making terrific sacrifices to come to this nation. Christian influences in our society have resulted in things like tolerance. The majority of the world is far less tolerant. The rights that have been given to women, children's rights, civil rights, the safe haven for immigrants—Christians have stood in the vanguard, the forefront, of all of those ideas as they influenced and changed our culture and society, and shaped our nation. Christians have led the fight for the poor, for children, for women, and for the abolition of slavery.

It's very important that we understand tolerance and freedom do not stand alone. They are not ideals that have the infrastructure to support themselves. They require a framework of values, and it's the Judeo-Christian faith that has provided such a framework for our nation for more than 200 years.

What separates the United States from so many cultures of the world is the influence of our Christian faith. I know it's chic these days to mock it, to denigrate it, to try to separate it from the public square, but in order to sell that message to the general population, you have to strip us of our history and pray that we're so ignorant we won't wake up and listen to what is being said, because it does take a rewriting of our story. We assume that our attitude of inclusivity and tolerance is a worldwide attitude. I assure you it is not. In the majority of the world, the poor, women, children, minority groups, the powerless—they're tyrannized. Now, our nation is not perfect, but if we neglect or set aside the value sets which spawned our freedoms, I assure you our freedoms will not persist. And if the Church isn't willing to stand up and be an advocate for our faith and for our Lord, those values will be swept out of our culture, out of our schools, and off our college campuses. We have been given the assignment to be salt and light.

If you can tolerate just a moment or two more, I'll give you a brief walk through some history. Harriet Beecher Stowe—perhaps you know the name. She wrote a book that influenced the direction of our country. She was the daughter of Lyman Beecher. He was a Presbyterian minister. She was so deeply impressed with a book she had read, Theodore Weld's, *Slavery as It Is*, that she wrote *Uncle Tom's Cabin*. In it, she struck at a national conscience in the hope that a cleansing of the nation's soul would avert a divine, public scourging of our nation.

Child labor reform was championed by the church. In the 1800's, children were put to work in the stifling hot and unbearably noisy factories as the Industrial Revolution began. They were kept in miserable places, treated as if they were soulless, and suffered under cruel discipline. There were no safety regulations. Financial penalties and even physical beatings were imposed for the slightest mistake or misdemeanor. Accidents and deaths were frequent. Children worked in factories 14 hours per day. They worked in mines, and were often asked to crawl through spaces that adults couldn't tolerate. Children worked on farms and in fields—enduring brutal labor, with little or no pay—until the Christian church, Christian worldview, intervened and said that they had to be treated with the dignity of humans.

The Civil Rights movement of the 1960's was a movement that was born in the churches. Dr. Martin Luther King, Jr. was a minister. He said, "We must keep God in the forefront. Let us be Christian in all our actions."

Immigration is another topic we hear a lot about these days. It's not new to our nation. We are a nation comprised of immigrants, but in order for us to live together, we have to live under the rule of law, and that requires a process for immigration. In the late 19th and early 20th centuries, America was faced with a massive wave of immigrants flooding into the cities. One estimate is that in 1914, one in three Americans was an immigrant or the child of an immigrant—one in three. There were multiple cities across our nation where the foreign-born outnumbered the native-born, two to one. Yet, a common faith held us together, not universally shared, but shared in a significant enough way and transferred from person to person and people group to people group. This faith gave us a common set of values that allowed the ideals of our nation (which were here from the beginning) to be extended from generation to generation. Today, these values and ideals continue to bring liberty and freedoms that we had not experienced in the nations from which we were fleeing.

II. A BATTLE FOR THE HEART & SOUL OF AMERICA — WHAT SHOULD WE DO?

Again, it's a distortion of reality to suggest that the liberties and freedoms we know are global. You and I are watching the twenty-first century edition of this challenge, and if you haven't realized it yet, I assure you there is a battle underway for the heart and soul of America. So, "What should we do? How do we respond? Do we say, "I'm just an individual. Nobody knows my name, or pays attention to me. I don't have access to great power or resources." What should we do?"

A. GIVE ATTENTION TO A RIGHT RELATIONSHIP WITH GOD

I'd like to politely push back on those responses for just a moment. You have access to the Creator of Heaven and Earth. Your names are known in the halls of Heaven. There are angels that have been dispatched at your disposal. We aren't just church attenders, or religionists, or ethicists, or moralists. We are children of the King, and we are on an assignment. I would submit that we need to begin by giving attention to a right relationship with God, not presuming upon it in arrogance and self-righteousness, imagining that we have done everything that should be done, but giving our full attention to developing a right relationship with God. He is the one who will bring promotion to our lives. If we will honor Him, as individuals, as families, as a nation, God will continue to promote us. If we dishonor Him, we will find ourselves with God as an adversary. In 1 Peter, the fisherman helps us with this:

> *Humble yourselves, therefore, under God's mighty hand, that he may lift you up in due time. Cast all your anxiety on him because he cares for you. Be self-controlled and alert. Your enemy the devil prowls around like a roaring lion looking for someone to devour. Resist him, standing firm in the faith, because you know that your brothers throughout the world are undergoing the same kind of sufferings.*

1 PETER 5:6-9

Peter is reminding us that we have an adversary. Again, not a particularly popular idea to hold—that there is someone who stands in opposition to God's purposes in your life. You know this. You experience it on a daily basis—in your thoughts, in your emotions, in your carnal self, in all sorts of external expressions around you. The decision to honor God, to choose God, to do the best you know before God, does not go unchallenged in your life.

How do we humble ourselves? Peter said to "humble ourselves under God's mighty hand." Humility is something that is acquired indirectly. You can't order it online. You can't go to the big box stores and pick it up. Humility develops within you, while you're occupied with something else. If Peter, nearing the end of his life, thought that humbling ourselves under God's mighty hand was the first step in God's program for our promotion, we need to understand it.

B. AN ASSIGNMENT FOR GOD'S PEOPLE

I believe I can hand you a key to self-humbling in the sight of God. I want to go back to the Old Testament. It's Leviticus, chapter 16. God is about to give an assignment to His people through Moses. In fact, God commands Moses to give an announcement to the people:

> "This shall be a statute forever for you: In the seventh month, on the tenth day of the month, you shall afflict your souls, and do no work at all, whether a native of your own country or a stranger who dwells among you. For on that day the priest shall make atonement for you, to cleanse you, that you may be clean from all your sins before the LORD. It is a sabbath

of solemn rest for you, and you shall afflict your souls. It is a
statute forever."

LEVITICUS 16:29-31 • NKJV®

God, through Moses, is giving an assignment to the Jewish people. He's telling them to celebrate on an annual basis—year after year forever—a special day. If they intend to be identified as the people of God, they are to pause and recognize the Day of Atonement. Some of you will know it by its Hebrew title, Yom Kippur. The Jewish people, from that day until this, and for more than 3,400 years or so, have honored the celebration known as the Day of Atonement. They kept the Day of Atonement when they were in concentration camps. The kept the Day of Atonement when they were dispersed through the nations of the world. The language that Moses used when he made the announcement is worth just a moment's attention. He said, "You shall afflict your souls." He said, "This is a statute forever," as in never to be released. It's not about your location, or the language you speak, or economic status, or whether you're blessed or you're struggling. It's a statute forever that "you should afflict your souls." Some of the modern translations will say "humble yourself."

In Acts 27:9, when the Day of Atonement is referenced by the Apostle Paul, he said it's just simply referred to as the Fast: "Much time had been lost, and sailing had already become dangerous because by now it was after the Fast." It's capitalized because the audience reading that in the book of Acts understood they were talking about the Day of Atonement.

So what is fasting? In its simplest definition, it is "abstaining from food for spiritual purposes." It means you miss a meal, not to shrink your waistline, but in pursuit of God. God said to His people that if you don't do this on an annual basis, you're no longer My people. It's a way of cultivating humility in your life.

Why does fasting have anything to do with our spiritual condition? I think to understand that, we have to understand a bit about the function of our soul. We are complex persons. You are a spirit. You live in a body, and you have a soul. Your body is temporary. That rascal is wearing out. You were born with an expiration date. Isn't that annoying? If you haven't had enough birthdays yet to figure that out, just hang on. Your soul has some very specific functions. Your soul, as it is generally described, houses your will, your intellect, and your emotions—that part of your person that responds to life with "I want," "I think," and "I feel," and those are powerful, powerful forces in your personality. Our soul is arrogant and self-assertive. The Bible coaches us that if we are going to live in the blessing of God, we have to learn to subdue our selfish soul—to say that what I want, and what I think, and what I feel will not dominate the course of my life. In Moses' language, we have to subdue our soul. To afflict our souls, we have to bring them under God's authority, under God's discipline. David understood it. In Psalm 35, verse 13, he said, "But as for me, when they were sick, my clothing was sackcloth;

I humbled my soul with fasting." Putting on sackcloth was an outward expression of humility when you were mourning or grieving.

The Bible tells us that David was a man after God's own heart, and yet he was a man with many weaknesses. Some of his failures were monumental, and he faced many challenges, both within his own family and his family system, and externally. From the moment that God gave David an assignment, there was a consistent challenge before him. In spite of all of the mistakes David made, God said that he is "a man after My own heart" (Acts 13:22).

"I humbled my soul with fasting." David understood how to humble his soul. I believe it's what kept him. And I'm submitting to you that it's a lesson that you and I need to learn. Not in theory. It will be necessary if we're going to respond to the greatest challenge we have seen in decades in our nation— far more threatening than 9/11, this season we're walking through. This isn't some external challenge that we can identify as an enemy combatant and then mobilize to stand against it. The challenges we're facing these days are coming from multiple fronts, and they are within us, within our own hearts. And the only way through this is to cooperate with Almighty God. He is the only one that can bring deliverance, freedom, and clarity to the confusion, and dispel the fears.

What I'd like to invite you to do is to join me for a season of fasting. In fact, I want to ask you to join me on a three day fast. You can fast in a way that is most appropriate to you—a way that is appropriate for your health, for your family responsibilities, for your own experience with fasting. You don't want to fast three days without food or water. You want to stay hydrated. Again, make the choices that are healthy for you. If fasting is a part of your spiritual discipline, maybe that three day period of time is something that you can embrace. If it's something that is new to you, maybe you simply want to take a meal each of those three days. Use the time that you would normally spend in preparing and enjoying a meal, and take that time with your Bible out and offer your prayers to God. Again, don't put yourself at risk, or others that you are responsible for. Allow the Spirit of God to direct you. I want to invite you to another opportunity. Would you consider doing a three day fast the first week of every month until we see God deliver us from this season of confusion, fear and division? I believe God will respond to us. I believe that's more powerful than anything being done in a laboratory. I believe that holds greater potential for our release and our prosperity than any plan the economists can make. I believe it will have a greater impact on the destiny of our nation than all of the political maneuvering that is taking place in this season.

As the Church of Jesus Christ, if we don't imagine that we have a place of authority and responsibility, then it becomes easy for the politicians to say that we're non-essential and recommend we lock the buildings. If we believe that the Creator of Heaven and Earth has called us to be difference-makers in a season such as this, then we will not relent.

III. BIBLICAL EXPRESSIONS OF FASTING

I want to give you a brief overview of some of the biblical expressions of fasting. This is not some subtle theme of Scripture.

A. UPON THE DEATH OF SAUL & JONATHAN

1 Samuel 31 is the last chapter of 1 Samuel, and verse 13 is the last verse. In Israel's war against the Philistines, King Saul and his son, Jonathan, were killed in battle on the same day. It was a transition in the nation of Israel, and it's a transition in the context of Scripture:

They took their bones and buried them under a tamarisk tree at Jabesh Gilead, and they fasted seven days.

1 SAMUEL 31:13

It feels like such a simple sentence. In fact, it's easy to just blow past it if you're doing your reading and you're on any kind of a timeline, or you've got some objective you're working toward. "They came and took the bones of Saul and Jonathan, and they fasted for seven days." It was an agrarian society. They were farmers. They worked with their hands. They had crops to tend, cattle to care for. They couldn't afford to sequester themselves in the house and rest, and yet they fasted for seven days. If you take a step back from that verse, I would submit to you that that single verse is more than a transition between books. It's a transition point in the unfolding of Scripture. 1 Samuel—it's a book about decline, division, and defeat. The Philistines have defeated Israel. The Israelites have fled eastward. At the end of that book, David's still living as a fugitive. His camp has been raided, the families and their possessions have been carried away, and David's own men are speaking of killing him. 2 Samuel is an entirely different book. It's a book about recovery, reunion, and victory. It seems to me that the transition point, the hinge, between those two narratives and the two different directions, is that one simple little sentence about the men of Jabesh Gilead: "they fasted for seven days."

B. JONAH

I'll give you another example, a familiar story from the book of Jonah. You know Jonah as a prophet, sometimes a non-prophet. You know his story, so I won't belabor it. God gave Jonah an assignment to go to Nineveh and to preach and tell the people that God's judgment was coming upon the city, but Jonah didn't want Nineveh to be spared. He wanted Nineveh to be destroyed. He was an astute enough observer of the rising of nations to know that Nineveh presented the greatest threat to his own people, and he wanted God's judgment to fall upon them. So Jonah refused the assignment and went the other way.

May I ask you a question? Do you imagine that when God presents you with an assignment—with an awareness of something that He is inviting you towards—that you have the luxury of just saying to the Creator of all things, "No, thank You." Well, God has given us a free choice. You and I have a free will. It separates us from all of creation. It should be a frightening thing to take the invitations of God—when you recognize He's inviting you to repentance, or to baptism, or to generosity, or to serving, or whatever it may be—and ignore and decline it. Do you imagine that that goes without consequence?

You see, I think we've been coached into a very lazy form of Christianity that invites us to recite a prayer, and yield our heart to the Lordship of Jesus Christ, and then rise from that point of prayer and perhaps we're dipped in a pool, and beyond that we imagine God has no further claims on our time, or our interest, or our attention. In fact, we imagine quite the opposite: now, we can command God where He should pay attention. That's worse than error. It's blasphemous. We are servants of the most High God with every day that He gives us breath. God wasn't created to do our bidding. We were created by Him to do *His*.

After Jonah had a little fishing adventure, he finally got to the City of Nineveh:

> *On the first day, Jonah started into the city. He proclaimed: "Forty more days and Nineveh will be overturned." The Ninevites believed God. They declared a fast, and all of them, from the greatest to the least, put on sackcloth. When the news reached the king of Nineveh, he rose from his throne, took he off his royal robes, and covered himself with sackcloth and he sat down in the dust. Then he issued a proclamation in the city: "By the decree of the king and his nobles: Do not let any man or beast, herd or flock, taste nothing. Let man and beast be covered with sackcloth. Let everyone call urgently on God. Let them give up their evil ways and their violence. Who knows? God may yet relent and with compassion turn from his fierce anger so that we will not perish."*
>
> JONAH 3:4-9

They had one message from a foreigner—somebody, that if he spoke their language, spoke it with an accent. They had no reason to trust him. They had no reason to listen to him. They had no reason to cooperate with him. In fact, it's inexplicable from just a logical, rational approach to the text. Yet, from the least to the greatest, the inhabitants of Nineveh repented.

When God saw what they did and how they turned from

their evil ways, he had compassion and did not bring upon
them the destruction he had threatened.

JONAH 3:10

Some of you are stuck. You worship your intellect. Now, I like
education. I could have been a professional student. I like to
learn and to read, and I'm quite happy in the stacks of books in
a library. But I had to learn to yield my intellect to God. He is
smarter than we are. Some of you think, *I don't have any idea why*
missing a meal would have any impact on the destiny of a nation,
or on my own personal trajectory, or my own spiritual life. Apart
from the Word of God and the counsel it gives us, we wouldn't
have any idea. But God spared a city because the people
humbled themselves in prayer and fasting, and changed their
ways. Nineveh was spared for more than 100 years. In fact, in a
startling contrast, Northern Israel did not repent—refused the
calls to repentance that came from multiple prophets. Nineveh
had one prophet from a foreign nation, and when they heard the
assignment the first time, they humbled themselves in fasting
and prayer. Northern Israel refused to do that under the tutelage
of multiple prophets, and Nineveh was the agent that God used
to discipline Northern Israel.

C. ESTHER

I'll give you another example: Esther, a young Jewish woman, who coincidentally became the Queen of Persia. She had a very powerful position, but there was a threat to the Jewish people. In fact, the King had signed an edict that the Jews throughout his empire were to be slaughtered on an appointed day. Her cousin, Mordechai, who had reared her, sent a message to Esther, asking her to intercede for her people—at some significant personal risk.

> "Do not think that because you are in the king's house you alone of all the Jews will escape. For if you remain silent at this time, relief and deliverance for the Jews will arise from another place, but you and your father's family will perish. And who knows but that you have come to royal position for such a time as this?"

ESTHER 4:13-14

You know, again it's probably worth noting, it's just a matter of history, that when Israel was free and independent, and they were given multiple warnings to repent or destruction would come, they refused the warnings. But when Israel lost their place in the land and their temple was destroyed, and they were living as exiles in foreign nations, on multiple occasions we watched the people of God respond to His invitations to humble themselves, and fast, and pray. When they

were in captivity, they were willing to cooperate with
God in a new way.

I took a moment with that because it seems to have
a parallel to us. We still have a good degree of our
independence. We still have freedom and liberty
to gather and worship, to come and go, and to use
our resources as we choose. I think the question
that is outstanding is will those of us who imagine
ourselves to be a part of the Body of Christ, will we
humble ourselves and repent, or will we imagine
that the problems that vex us are the responsibility
of the wicked?

Look at Esther's answer to Mordechai:

*"Go, gather together all the Jews who are in Susa, and fast
for me. Do not eat or drink for three days, night or day. I and
my maids will fast as you do. When this is done, I will go to
the king, even though it is against the law. And if I perish,
I perish."*

ESTHER 4:16

Until this day, the Jewish people celebrate that victory. It's
known as the Jewish holiday, Purim. God responded to the
people when they humbled themselves, when they afflicted their

souls. The one who had instigated the annihilation was himself destroyed, along with the plans he had made for the people. God supernaturally intervened. Do you believe that God intervenes in the course of human history? It's important, Church. Why would we trust science more than we trust God? And I'm not against science. I'm grateful for all the work scientists do, but the Church has to believe that Almighty God has a stronger hand than any force that a human being can initiate.

I want to finish the story. I think it's relevant:

> *On the third day Esther put on her royal robes and stood in the inner court of the palace, in front of the king's hall. The king was sitting on his royal throne in the hall, facing the entrance. When he saw Queen Esther standing in the court, he was pleased with her and held out to her the gold scepter that was in his hand. So Esther approached and touched the tip of the scepter.*
>
> ESTHER 5:1-2

After Esther had fasted and prayed for three days, she put on her royal robes and went to see the king. If you went without a summons, and the king didn't lower his scepter to welcome you, you'd be executed. It was a harsh time. After Esther and all those who attended her, and all those who would stand with her, prayed and fasted; she put on her royal robes. I have an image of that. She is standing there as the Queen, dressed in her royal finery. I love the image because I want to suggest an image to you. After we have humbled ourselves, and we have repented, we have to put on our royal robes and present ourselves to the King. If we intend to change history, fasting, prayer, and repentance is our pathway. Listen to the prophet, Isaiah:

> *I delight greatly in the LORD; my soul rejoices in my God.*
> *For he has clothed me with garments of salvation and arrayed*
> *me in a robe of righteousness, as a bridegroom adorns his head*
> *like a priest, and as a bride adorns herself with her jewels.*

ISAIAH 61:10

We have to humble ourselves and understand we stand in the righteousness that is ours in Christ. We stand clothed—not in our own self-righteousness—but with the glorious provision of the redemptive work of God. When we stand in this way, we can come boldly, the author of Hebrews says, before the throne of grace, and find mercy to help us in our time of need. We have an assignment, Church, and it's to be more than spectators, who consume the news, and fill our hearts with anguish and panic.

D. EZRA

I'll give you one more example: Ezra, a priest. He's in exile, and he's commissioned by the Persian king to lead a group of exiles to return to Jerusalem. He's entrusted with all of the hardware from the Temple, the serving dishes and all the things that were necessary. They're made out of gold, silver, and other precious metals. He's traveling with tremendous wealth, and he's anxious. He's got to make a difficult trip of several hundred miles, along trade routes that are occupied by thieves and brigands. Ezra makes an important decision:

> *There, by the Ahava Canal, I proclaimed a fast, so that we might humble ourselves before our God and ask him for a safe journey for us and our children, with all our possessions.*

> EZRA 8:21

Isn't that what we're asking God for—a safe journey through this season of disruption and confusion and fear, for ourselves and for all who are traveling with us and our children? Ezra said:

> *I was ashamed to ask the king for soldiers and horsemen to protect us ... we had told the king, "The gracious hand of our God is on everyone who looks to him...." So we fasted and petitioned our God about this, and he answered our prayer.*

> EZRA 8:22-23

This is relevant to our history. Our nation was birthed by a group of men and women who committed themselves to unite in prayer and fasting. You've heard of the Pilgrims? We have a holiday where they still get some partial billing, right?

Remember the Pilgrims? They had buckles on their shoes and turkeys on their tables. The Pilgrims emerged from a sect within England, the Puritans. I don't have time to unpack the differences and the distinctions, but William Bradford and the Pilgrims who helped found this nation were consistently united in public prayer and fasting. It was a part of their lives, privately and publicly.

I'll give you one example. I could have brought many because it's a part of William Bradford's writings. They were about to depart on the journey to cross the ocean. It says, "Being ready to depart, they had a day of solemn humiliation. Their pastor, John Robinson, took his text from Ezra 8:21." Sound familiar? "By the Ahava Canal, I proclaimed a fast, so that we might humble ourselves before our God and ask him for a safe journey for us and our children, with all our possessions."

Bradford goes on to write, "Upon which Robinson spent a good part of the day very profitably and suitable to their present occasion. The rest of the time was spent in pouring out prayers to the Lord with great fervency mixed with the abundance of tears" *.

Did you know our nation was birthed by a group of people who stood together in prayer and fasting before they faced the challenges of their lives? That's our history. The practice of setting aside special days of prayer and fasting became an accepted

---

* *Excerpted from the book, The Rewriting of America's History © 1990 by Catherine Millard*

part of life in the Plymouth Colony. On November 15, 1636, a law was passed that allowed the governor and his assistants to command, "Solemn days of humiliation by fasting, and also for thanksgiving as the occasion shall be offered." What we're doing today is not a deviation from our history. We're asking God for His blessing, for His guidance, for His deliverance upon us in this season of our history together. We refuse to simply consume the blessings of the sacrifices of those who have gone before us. We'll take our place as the people of God in this generation.

E. JESUS

Now, I'm sure there's a skeptic or two saying, "Pastor, those are all Old Testament examples." You're right, Obi-Wan. So let me give you one New Testament example, from a figure I think you'll know. His name is Jesus:

> *Jesus, full of the Holy Spirit, returned from the Jordan and was led by the Spirit in the desert, where for forty days he was tempted by the devil. He ate nothing during those days, and at the end of them he was hungry.*
>
> LUKE 4:1-2

Jesus did not begin His public ministry until He had spent 40 days seeking God with prayer and fasting. If it was important for the sinless, obedient Son of God—sent to the earth, incarnate, on an assignment to seek and to save those who were lost (Luke 19:10)—if it was necessary for Him to fast and pray to fulfill God's assignment for His life, can you imagine that it might be relevant for you and me?

In fact, in that same chapter of Luke's Gospel, it says that after this time of temptation and fasting, His ministry begins:

> *Jesus returned to Galilee in the power of the Spirit, and news about him spread through the whole countryside. He taught in their synagogues, and everyone praised him.*
>
> LUKE 4:14-15

Jesus' ministry is launched. It goes viral, if we can borrow a term. "He returned in the power of the Spirit." I think the distinction between being filled with the Spirit, and leading a life in the power of the Spirit, has to do with our determination to afflict our souls—to humble ourselves, and fast, and seek the face of the Lord. I know many Christians who imagine themselves Spirit-filled, and they'll give you evidence in their prayer lives, or their prayer languages, or many expressions of that. But there is a difference in saying, "I'm filled with the Spirit," and leading a life in the power of the Spirit of God. We need the power of the Spirit of God to be displayed in this season. Our churches have been inert for too long. If we will subdue our soulish self and give first place to the Spirit of God, the power of the Spirit will manifest Himself in our presence.

IV. THE POWER OF REPENTANCE

I want to extend an invitation, and I'd like to highlight the power of repentance in our lives. You see, repentance unleashes belief, and faith, and faithfulness in us. We've been watching, of late, demonstrations in the streets of our cities, and we've heard calls from multiple fronts for others to repent. It seems to me there is a high degree of consciousness, awareness, of the sins of other people, and even the sins of other generations. But it seems also to me that we are much less concerned with our own heart condition and our own obedience to God. We can't repent for others, but we can repent for ourselves.

When Jesus began His ministry, the Bible records that He went into Galilee and proclaimed the good news of God:

> *After John was put in prison, Jesus went into Galilee, proclaiming the good news of God. "The time has come," he said. "The kingdom of God is near. Repent and believe the good news!"*

<u>MARK 1:14-15</u>

Repentance is the catalyst. It's the accelerant for belief. If you are struggling to believe, if there are places where doubt and skepticism hold a place in your thoughts and your emotions, repentance is your path to freedom. Perhaps you doubt that the blood of Jesus is sufficient to set you free—that you have failed so gloriously, and so magnificently, and so frequently that you're relegated to the second class citizenry of the Kingdom. Or perhaps your battle is elsewhere. You feel like you would have to lower yourself to believe the Word of God to be inspired, authoritative, and directive. Our adversary is clever, and he'll put us in bondage with whatever lie we're willing to listen to, but if we will pause and invite the Holy Spirit into our lives with the spirit of humility and repentance, the barriers to belief will crumble. You'll be able to believe where you have stood as a staunch skeptic. Whatever the source may be, whatever avenue it has taken, Jesus gave us the formula: repent and believe. One last verse of advice:

> *Sow for yourselves righteousness, reap the fruit of unfailing love, and break up your unplowed ground; it is time to seek the LORD, until he comes and showers righteousness on you.*

HOSEA 10:12

What we're asking God to do is come by His Spirit and shower righteousness upon our nation—in our homes, in our schools, on our college campuses, in the Halls of Congress, in our hospital corridors. Would you not put your face on the ground and weep to see righteousness showered upon our nation? The prophet gives us the pathway. He said that we have to break up our unplowed ground. Some of the older translations say, "our fallow ground"—the ground that may have been fruitful in earlier seasons, but it's been left untilled, untended. It was treated presumptively. It was ignored, and now it has to be broken up again. Repentance is the catalyst for that.

Now, I know if you've been around church twice, you're familiar with the word *repent*. But I honestly don't believe you can be a faithful disciple of Jesus unless you're very much familiar and at home with the practice of repentance. Repentance isn't something that the pagans need to do. Repentance is the practice of the people of God.

I want to invite you towards a different attitude towards repentance in your life. Don't be in a hurry with it. Ask the Spirit of God to help you to thoroughly examine the state of your heart and see what condition you're in. Check to see if on a daily basis you are walking with God, or if you're walking with the devil. You may need to break your day into segments. Do you honor God throughout the course of your day? I don't mean for you to simply glance at your past life and acknowledge that it was filled with sin and ungodliness, and then go to God with a general confession, and just dump the whole lot on the ground. That's not what I'm suggesting. I'm asking you to look at each individual thing that the Spirit of God brings to your mind, one at a time. Take a pen and paper, perhaps. You know, I'm grateful for technology. I use a computer a lot, but if I'm really getting serious about something, I want a legal pad and a pen. I like lists. Whatever tool is most comfortable in your hand, take some time. Ask the Spirit of God to help you think of your failures, your sins. Don't ignore them. There is a solution for them. There is a remedy for them. Ignoring them, denying them, and hiding them in the past, or the recesses of your memory, doesn't bring freedom. Go over what the Spirit reveals to you carefully as if you were evaluating a bill or a receipt. Each time something else comes to mind, put it on the list.

A. SINS OF OMISSION

I want to expand the way you think of sin. Don't simply think about the sins you have committed. Think about the things you have failed to do. You rather casually say, "Oh, those are sins of omission." God looks upon them with grace. That attitude is a bit casual for me. Sins of omission are the things we fail to do.

I'll give you an example. We fail so often to be thankful. We are a uniquely blessed people. We have food, clothing, and shelter. Our children have medicine, food to eat, and educational opportunities available to them. We have the freedom to travel, to make decisions, to self-direct our lives in a way few people on planet Earth have ever had—and we're reluctant to give thanks to God. We say things like: "You know, I'm just not emotional. I'm not expressive. I'm more of an introvert." Or, "I prefer to worship God internally." We have all kinds of reasons why we stand in our own ingratitude and stubborn selfishness, and not say, "God, thank You for what You've done in my life. I could have been born in some distant place without access to electricity. Only Your grace and Your mercy has made this possible for me."

There are many ways that we fail to respond to God, which is really a lack of love for Him. We neglect our Bibles. We have the privilege of having the Word of God available to us, and our typical default response is, "How much do I have to read? And how often do I have to read it, and do I have to read it again? The words are hard." Typically, we don't respond with a sense of gratitude and appreciation that the Word of God is available to us. Without it, we would know nothing of the character of God.

Another area is our lack of concern for unbelievers. It's easier to be angry with them: "Why do they behave that way?" We neglect to care for one another.

B. OVERT SINS

The list we're more familiar with are the sins we commit overtly, our ungodly choices. I think the one that plagues this generation is worldliness, even within the Church. I think we have sold our souls to comfort, convenience, pride, and envy. It seems that our desire for more is insatiable. Contentment has escaped us because we're filled with covetousness and envy, a critical spirit, and a lack of respect. It's washing over us like an avalanche. Within the Church, we haven't even respected God. We practice lying. We've got a whole new set of vocabulary words for the frequency with which we lie. We spin things. We misremember. We say, "Well that's your truth." We cheat and we call it good business. If we find a way to make some inappropriate profit—because the person we're dealing with is either unaware or incapable of understanding what's beneath our profit—we don't imagine that we are cheating somebody for personal gain. We say, "We've done good business." God forgive us.

In all these things, I'm not talking about those beyond the Church. This is our hypocrisy. We rob God. We don't give. We find some story about someone misappropriating funds with which they were entrusted, and we think that relieves us from our obligation to lead generous lives. It seems that we have unleashed our tempers. We've given ourselves an emotional license. We've got a whole new vocabulary for that, too. Consider road rage. We used to call you a bad driver. Think about unforgiveness. The list goes on and on.

I want to ask you to consider joining me in a three-day fast. Choose the part that is appropriate for you, but I want to ask you if you'll take a step of faith with me in an expression of repentance. I know the Spirit of God has touched some of your hearts, and you're uncomfortable with the place you've stood, the things you've tolerated, and the things you've excused and justified. I have a prayer for you, but before we pray, I want to ask you if you have been convicted of that as you've been reading, I want to ask you if you would be willing to offer a prayer of repentance to the Lord.

I want to include in that another invitation. Evangelism in the New Testament always includes a demonstration of the power of God. We don't serve God just intellectually. We serve Him because we recognize that He is a God who delivers, and if you have a need—maybe you need healing, maybe somebody you care about does, there is some tremendous pressure in your life—we're going to ask God to bring health to your mortal bodies as we ask Him to cleanse us of our stubbornness, and our rebellion, and our sin. We're inviting the Spirit of God to begin a cleansing within us. Say, "God, I need your help." God responds to people who seek Him.

Pray this prayer:

Heavenly Father, forgive me for ignoring Your counsel and for choosing my own way. I have turned my back on You, on Your goodness, and abundant blessings. I have chosen pride and indulgence over righteousness and purity. I humble myself today in repentance and ask for Your mercy. We are a people and a nation in need of healing. Only You, Almighty God, can restore our fortunes. I cry out to You today for mercy. I do not blame others for my circumstances; I have walked this path. This day I acknowledge Almighty God as the Judge of all the earth. May the name of Jesus of Nazareth be lifted up in our homes, in our city, in our state, in our nation.

Holy Spirit, I ask You to guide me. If there are places where I have tolerated and accepted the things that have separated me

from Your best, I want to turn away from them. I want to lay them down. No excuses. No justifications. I want to separate myself from each of those things, today. I ask for Your mercy, Your cleansing, and Your forgiveness through the blood of Jesus. Holy Spirit, continue to speak to me far beyond this moment in time. Cleanse me and I will be clean. Deliver me and I will be delivered. Wash me and I will be made white again.

Lord, I pray for those with great needs. Some are facing sickness and disease, and I pray that in the name of Jesus You would restore their health. Bring life to their bodies. Where they have been weak, may they gain strength. Where they face challenges, Lord, I pray there will be resolutions available. In the name of Jesus, Father, let us begin to celebrate victories and wholeness in the Church and in our nation. Father, those who have struggled with oppression and depression, with heaviness and discouragement and addictions, in Jesus' Name, may those forces be broken over their lives this day. Through the blood of Jesus, we have been redeemed out of an empty way of life. We have been set free to serve a living God. I humble myself today. Our nation can't save or deliver itself, but through the blood of Jesus we have been redeemed, and I praise You for it this day. In Jesus' name. Amen.

NOTES

NOTES

NOTES

NOTES

NOTES

NOTES

NOTES

NOTES

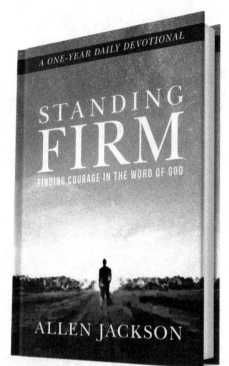

THREE-VOLUME SMALL GROUP VIDEO STUDY & GUIDE

THE WHITEBOARD BIBLE™

The Bible tells a story, and these small group studies will help you more fully understand it. The three volumes of *The Whiteboard Bible* develop a twelve-point timeline that serves as the framework for all the characters and events in the Bible, beginning with Creation and concluding with Jesus' return.

For more from Allen Jackson, including sermons, books, and small group materials, visit:

allenjackson.com

ABOUT THE AUTHOR

Allen Jackson is passionate about helping people become more fully devoted followers of Jesus Christ, who respond to God's invitations for their life.

He has served World Outreach Church since 1981, becoming senior pastor in 1989. Under his leadership, WOC has grown to a congregation of over 15,000 through outreach activities, community events, and worship services designed to share the gospel.

Through Allen Jackson Ministries™, his messages reach people across the globe—through television, radio, Sirius XM, and online streaming. His teachings are also available in published books and other resources.

With degrees from Oral Roberts University and Vanderbilt University, and additional studies at Gordon-Conwell Theological Seminary and Hebrew University of Jerusalem, Jackson is uniquely equipped to help people develop a love and understanding of God's Word.

Pastor Jackson's wife, Kathy, is an active participant in ministry at World Outreach Church.

CPSIA information can be obtained
at www.ICGtesting.com
Printed in the USA
LVHW052157181021
700736LV00007B/7

9 781617 180514